MW01713490

THE SELF FUNDING HOUSE™

Rebuilding the Dream of Home Ownership

Other Books by Derek Lobo

The Future Apartment Developer:
The Blueprint for Building Rental Apartments and Intergenerational Wealth (MPS-DALA, 2021)

A Field Guide to Rental Apartment Development by the Numbers:
Building and Testing a Detailed Financial Feasibility Model (MPS-DALA, 2021)

The Feasibility Study Determines the Apartment You Build:
How to Build the Right Apartment Building in the Right Location for the Right Resident (MPS-DALA, 2021)

Finding Money to Build Apartments:
Make Better Deals by Finding Cheaper Capital (MPS-DALA, 2021)

A Field Guide to Municipal Taxes and Operating Costs:
Decreasing Your Operating Costs to Maximize Value (MPS-DALA, 2021)

The Four Factors That Drive Rent:
Why $100 More in Rent = $24,000 in Increased Value (MPS-DALA, 2021)

Intensifying Existing Developments with Apartments:
Apartments Are the Most Profitable Additions When Intensifying Land (MPS-DALA, 2021)

Building Apartments with a Joint Venture Partner:
Structuring a Deal so That the Lender, Developer, and Partner Win (MPS-DALA, 2021)

Writing and Executing the Marketing Plan:
Strategies to Get Your Building Full at the Highest Rent (MPS-DALA, 2021)

Writing and Executing a Sales and Leasing Plan:
Hiring, Training, Managing, and Compensating Your Leasing Staff for Maximum Results (MPS-DALA, 2021)

Designing Apartments for the Future:
Meeting Modern Expectations with Innovative Design (MPS-DALA, 2021)

Becoming a Successful Merchant Apartment Builder:
Developing a Business Plan and Growing Your Wealth (MPS-DALA, 2021)

Finding and Acquiring Land for Apartment Development:
Processes for Site Selection Through Closing (MPS-DALA, 2021)

The Intentional Apartment Developer:
A Programmatic Guide for Planning, Designing, Building, Leasing, Managing, and Selling (DALA, 2022)

A Private Developer's Roadmap for Affordable Housing:
Profitable Rental Apartment Solutions in Canada (DALA, 2022)

America Needs More Apartments:
The Comprehensive Guide for Apartment Developers (DALA, 2022)

The Blueprint for Your Self Funding House™:
Everything Needed for Transforming Your Home into a Business (DALA, 2023)

Stakeholders of The Self Funding House™:
Coordination of Politicians, Lenders, Municipalities, and the Homeowner (DALA, 2023)

THE SELF FUNDING HOUSE™

Rebuilding the Dream of Home Ownership

DEREK LOBO
with ROD SCHULHAUSER

THE SELF FUNDING HOUSE™

THE SELF FUNDING HOUSE™
Rebuilding the Dream of Home Ownership

Derek Lobo
with Rod Schulhauser

Published by DALA Inc.

Derek Lobo
905-565-4428
derek.lobo@rockadvisorsinc.com
RockAdvisorsInc.com
TheSelfFundingHouseBook.com
Online Learning Portal: TheSelfFundingHouse.com.

ISBN:
Soft Cover: 978-1-998866-00-7
eBook: 978-1-998866-01-4

Printed in Canada
First Edition, February 2023

Editor & eBook Layout: Rory d'Eon
Proofreader: E.B.A.
Interior Layout: Adam Carter
Cover: Adam Carter
Project Management: Rod Schulhauser & DALA Inc.

Dedication

I dedicate this book to all the dreamers who believe in home ownership and want to be a part of solving the global housing crisis.

It's the right thing to do.

DEREK LOBO

Table Of Contents

Acknowledgments

There has never been a more important time to put out a book like this.

I would like to thank all those that have inspired me to write this message and all the readers who provided valuable feedback on the early manuscripts.

I also want to acknowledge the tremendous effort put forth by my team, Rod Schulhauser, Rory d'Eon, and Adam Carter. They have executed a fantastic process that allowed me to write this book within the framework of my busy entrepreneurial lifestyle.

I remain thankful for all our clients and collaborators. I also need to extend my continued appreciation to Dan Sullivan, whose mentorship and friendship have been pivotal in shaping my strategic thinking and opening new avenues for me to explore both at work and at home.

Thank you all!

Preface

"You can't go back and change the beginning, but you can start where you are and change the ending."
– C.S. Lewis

I'm a real estate practitioner who's been involved in real estate for many years. My career aspirations began around the age of eight years old as I sat with my parents at our dining room table. We were wondering how we would sublet our rental apartment that we had leased for one year, but then decided to move out after only eight months. I felt privileged to be included in this conversation and deeply moved, not only by the inclusion, but the process of planning how our future would unfold. This is where my enthusiasm for real estate as a career ignited.

Looking back, we had experienced firsthand, how valuable decent affordable housing was to us during those first years in our new country. For me, it drove home the point that secure and dependable affordable housing is a fundamental building block of our society—crucial in the formative years of a young person's life, and paving the way to continued success as a contributing member of society.

For our family, coming from another country and culture, moving here became a rebirth of sorts—our rental provided the needed housing stability. From it, we could start fresh, on our terms, secure in our space to familiarize ourselves with a new culture without the burden of housing instability. Some of you are in this kind of situation, some are not, but all new families need housing security to grow and become successful. This book's aim is to broaden the base of affordable housing, so it's not just developers providing rental housing, but anyone thinking seriously about creating rental housing while buying a home, either their first one or any subsequent purchase.

Over the years, with a thorough grasp of the housing affordability challenges we now face, years of experience with developers and apartment owners, and some valuable insights, I've come to believe that I have a duty to my new country, and the world at large, to disseminate what I've learned because it's the right thing to do. I believe that this book, and the others that will follow, will considerably ease a housing crisis that should never have occurred in the first place. I'd love for the entrepreneurial-minded individuals among you to take my message to heart and see where it takes you.

There's a huge opportunity awaiting. With the right mindset and some guidance, making home ownership self funding is entirely feasible and very rewarding. I urge as many of you as possible to consider buying a house-as-a-business so you can experience the thrill of home ownership, the potential of financial freedom, the opening of new career opportunities, and as a bonus, help solve our housing shortage.

It's the right thing to do.

Introduction

"My dream is to transform the housing market worldwide."
– Derek Lobo

If you're encountering housing affordability challenges and need a realistic path to home ownership and financial freedom, this book is for you. It focuses on rebuilding your dream of home ownership by adapting your mindset to face, then overcome, the challenges in today's housing market. You'll acquire a thorough understanding of the actionable steps to prepare yourself for potential home ownership and gain the confidence to turn your dream into reality with the right mindset to ensure success.

I'm targeting that individual who has a housing affordability challenge and is willing to consider accessory dwelling units (ADUs) as a source of extra income that will help buy that house.

By thinking differently and creatively, and using the principles of a shared economy, buying a house-as-a-business offers huge advantages, many of which you may not yet realize, but will definitely excite you. Not only does buying a house-as-a-business make financial freedom possible, it also opens the door to career opportunities in the real estate and development field.

Buying a house is not the same experience as it was a few decades ago. Prices have risen sharply while income has not kept pace. It's generated a palpable anxiety in potential home buyers. The fear of missing out is real. To alleviate that anxiety, I'm urging you to consider a house-buying model that reflects current conditions and offers a way to overcome the affordability obstacles of the current housing market so that you can become a proud homeowner.

This Book's Aim Is To Inspire You to Actually Do It

By adding ADUs, you'll be helping yourself and others as well—the leadership you provide will be an example for others to follow (along with adding valuable new affordable housing). While this may sound unrealistic to some, I don't apologize for thinking this way. I know the process works—I've done it. Many are doing it today; many have done so in the past. Now, so can you. Others who have seen me go through the process have gone on to duplicate that success for themselves.

I'd like to see a new wave of homeowners who want to realize the business value of their houses. I encourage new buyers to get into the home developer business even if it's just using their own home. As you may know, most real estate developers got their start with just a single house, often their own.

From there, I want to teach the world how to build rental apartments. I want to become the *Developer of Developers*. Just think how many potential developers could be spurred into action if they knew how well this process works. Could a housing revolution be created by a new wave of enterprising housing entrepreneurs, some of whom will become wildly successful? I would love to see that!

Online Learning Portal for creating your **Self Funding House™**

The current housing shortage is a relatively new problem. Ten years ago, this problem did not exist. The problem is compounded by the fact that the traditional way of buying a home is now broken. So, not only is there a new problem, but the solution is unknown—or at least fairly murky—to many of you. And the only way forward is to resolve it. I feel it's my duty to disseminate this innovative and exciting solution as widely as possible to get you prepared and enthusiastic so you can make your dream a reality.

How I Came to This Conclusion

I've spent my entire life working in the apartment business. I've leased, managed, and sold apartment buildings my entire life—of all qualities and sizes. Typically, but not always, renters are in a lower income bracket—less than the average homeowner. Some of the situations I've encountered are less than optimal, sometimes disturbing. I've witnessed poverty, which broke my heart. It's made me realize the importance of housing availability, which is driven by supply. If you create more supply, there will be more choice, rental costs will decrease, renters will benefit, and so will society.

If you're a homeowner, the housing supply shortage works in your favor. For a potential owner, house prices are high, but when they build accessory dwelling units (ADUs), they'll be able to get quality tenants while providing good rental rates due to that shortage.

As an immigrant, I know firsthand how important decent affordable housing was to my life, my family, and our chances of success in later years. In my 20s, I became a net producer of apartments by adding two more units to a house I'd just purchased. So, I helped myself by buying a house I wouldn't have been able to afford had it not been for the rental income. In the process, I created two new apartments that others could live in. But more than that, I felt the pride of becoming a homeowner, and I could offer decent accommodations to my tenants.

The combination of my early life as an immigrant, buying a house I couldn't normally afford, then meeting holocaust survivors who built all those apartments in the 1950s and '60s so that my family, and others like us had a place to live—had a profound impact on what I am doing now. It all came full circle to my idea that, as housing prices rose and affordability became a problem, I figured there had to be a solution in there somewhere.

My family came to this country and moved into one of those apartments. I sometimes joke and say, "I read my first lease when I was eight years old." That's because I helped my parents sublet it.

What Is the Housing Affordability Solution?

I've studied all the solutions being proposed. Many were too expensive. Others weren't viable, or would take a decade before having any meaningful impact. Finally, my thinking evolved to: *what's the biggest, fastest, cheapest, and easiest way to solve the housing shortage?*

I came up with this:

- **BIGGEST**: millions of existing homes, and future homes, could be converted to include more housing units.
- **FASTEST**: it wouldn't take that long (relatively) to do the conversions.
- **CHEAPEST**: those conversions only cost a percentage of the house's value to build.
- **EASIEST**: This is not a complex solution, unlike solving something like climate change—this is solvable now with resources we already have and long-existing technology and skills.

This solves the too expensive, too difficult, and too long-to-implement issues. It also introduces the concept of solving the housing shortage with a shared economy approach.

UBERIZING THE HOME

Think about Uber or any ride share service. If you own a car, you can monetize that car—or buy a better car—by using it to generate an income. Driving it gets you out of the house, allowing you to meet interesting people. It also provides you with a job—either full-time or part-time. The concept is simple: you're using your car as a business rather than something that serves only yourself.

That same approach—thinking of the house as a business, instead of the traditional way—works for you when you want to buy a house, and for those who already own a house, and the renters who'll live in that house. You have the option of using this Uber model of renting out part of your house if you want to. The key is that it's financially viable—and that makes it very attractive. As the homeowner, conversion to an income-generating house allows you to keep the house while maintaining an income if you lose your job. The income from the ADUs may also allow you to buy a better house than you could otherwise afford.

As you may know, financially, multiple sources of income are always better than a single source. Had I lost my job due to layoffs or recession, the two units I rented would have let me keep the house and stay financially solvent. Adding an additional source of income brought resilience to my life.

So, without the risk of being a traditional business owner, without any employees, without customers (other than renters), or any stock turnover, I owned a successful business. In essence, in a short time, I'd come a long way towards attaining financial freedom. That path is available to you as well.

FORMALIZING THE PROCESS INTO A REPLICABLE MODEL

A traditional business, such as owning a restaurant, small manufacturing company, or retail, is not for everyone. There's a lot at play that many don't want to deal with. The related stress and long hours can take their toll. However, home ownership is something you understand and already participate in. The rules are clear and well understood.

Like starting a business with your car (think Uber again), you can begin a business with your house. Admittedly, Uberizing your house is more difficult than simply working with a car, but it's entirely doable with well-established conventions unlocking great potential gains.

Why Me? Why Now?

If you've picked up this book, you're already interested in, not only buying a house, but open to the idea of buying one with a view to its purpose and management being business focused. This is fundamentally different from the traditional buy, move-in, live there for a period, then maybe sell to buy a bigger or better-located house. You're intrigued by the financial reward potential a business unlocks along with the pride of ownership. Don't forget, ADUs create additional housing units easing the supply challenge.

I have decades of real estate experience to draw from. I know the market and I'm considered an expert in my niche. I also have children facing the current housing reality—as do many of my business associates. And I fully understand that today's housing reality is vastly different from when I bought my first triplex. However, my experience, relationships, and collaborators, all coupled with my entrepreneurial success, assures me that the solution I have is real and doable.

TheSelfFundingHouse.com

Assembling the knowledge, wisdom, and content from many collaborators and industry experts. This Online Learning Portal will address the basic steps and solutions to challenges for buying a home-as-a-business and creating your **Self Funding House™**.

1

Reality Requires Rethinking

"Have the courage to follow your heart and intuition. They somehow already know what you truly want to become. Everything else is secondary."
– Steve Jobs

My Mindset Foundation

I guess you could say my mindset was born out of necessity. Immersed into a new culture at a very young age, my first need was to learn how to think about myself and the situations and opportunities presented to me at the moment—not those from my past. In order to be successful, I had to believe that the decisions I made didn't impact my need for security and my drive to make a go of it.

After I graduated from college, I moved to another city for employment—and I needed a place to live. So, along with two other strangers (at first), I rented a room in a three-bedroom townhouse. Each of us paid $500 in rent. Which meant the landlord collected $1,500 in rent from which to pay his expenses. I found out later that the market value for that townhouse was $1,000. In effect, we were paying the landlord a $500 premium.

MY AHA MOMENT

My thought was that the landlord was playing his cards well. He was getting three tenants to pay off his mortgage and collecting a premium on top of market value. In addition, the landlord owned a second townhouse occupied by himself and other tenants, thus paying off that home from generated income as well. So, I figured he was financially set.

Once making a solid workman's income, I wanted a place of my own. I needed more privacy than a shared townhouse could provide. So, I tasked my real estate agent to find me a home, such as a duplex (also known as a secondary unit), so that I could emulate my landlord—having others pay my mortgage. He found a house that I could convert into a triplex.

That house was three times my income—inexpensive by today's standards. However, interest rates were far higher back then, driving my mortgage payments up. I renovated the home, added kitchens, doors, outside entrances, and whatever I needed to make it into a workable triplex—providing my own labor where possible to keep costs down. That cost me less than 5% of the cost of the house (I added my labor at no cost). Then, I moved into the basement. That house was my self funding house.

By taking the least desirable unit, I generated the highest income possible. I set myself a goal of paying off my mortgage in five years by using the rental income to pay down as much principal as I could. By doing this, I had created a solid footing in the housing market for myself.

TAKING THE HOUSE BUSINESS TO THE NEXT LEVEL

While living there, I began dating a woman who, shortly after, became my wife. After we married, she moved in with me—making her the target of some good-natured comments about finally moving up in the world—into a basement. Had we been married and then attempted to convert a home into a triplex—with the proviso that she moves into the basement with me—she may have considered that too risky a situation. My dream of making my home a business may have been derailed. My wife had her own mindset shift when she understood what I had accomplished and what I had to offer—I came with a basement apartment in a triplex as well as financial security.

MANY OF US HAVE LIVED IN AN APARTMENT—LIKELY, YOU HAVE AS WELL

Many of us have been tenants living with tenant neighbors all around us. Nothing bad happened because of it. It's my belief that the fear of having unsafe tenants is unfounded. Ask yourself the following questions: *Does the Uber driver worry about who they're picking up? Do we trash cars when we rent them? Does the hotel owner worry about destroyed rooms?*

Most tenants do not destroy the apartments they live in. They want to live peacefully as much as you do. It is a consumer/provider relationship, both going about their jobs well. The quality of your tenants is tied directly to the quality of your rental unit and the rent that you charge. As to the risks of having tenants move out, they eventually did, necessitating a search for replacements. I quickly learned how to process turnover properly to assure myself that whomever I rented to was decent and trustworthy. Our Self Funding House™ online learning portal provides information to help you vet potential tenants.

What It Did for Me

That house allowed me, a single guy with a modest income, to enter into the housing market. Then, it allowed me to bring in a spouse and grow a family. Later, when I started my own business, the basement became my office. And since the basement had an outside entrance, we had room left over for a nanny apartment.

This house, that adventure, was my entrepreneurial start in life. I had been just a regular guy working at a factory who had to learn to negotiate real estate purchasing, convert a house into apartments, find appropriate tenants, collect rents, do my income taxes, maintain, and pay house expenses, and keep everyone happy—including myself. That took some effort, but I was able to buy a house that I couldn't otherwise afford and pay it off faster than the normal 25-year mortgage term. I was thrilled and felt empowered to be where I was in life.

It Will Empower You Too

If you've come this far into the book, you've given a great deal of thought into finding a way to buy a home. I'm here to tell you that it is possible if you think differently than your parents and are willing to treat your home as a business. And I'm well aware that shifting mindsets is difficult, especially if the mindset you're trying to reach is rather vague.

THIS BOOK DESCRIBES THIS TARGET MINDSET

Shifting your mindset is impactful for you, your family, and others who rent from you, but also impactful for society. It's my belief that the sooner the general population realizes that decent, affordable housing is a necessity, the sooner the housing crisis will recede.

I want you to consider all the possibilities that home ownership-as-a-business opens up for you. The pride of owning your first home cannot be overstated, and the potential financial gains are immense. Many careers have begun this way. Mine has and so have that of countless landlords and developers. Yours can too.

The potential rewards you'll miss by not taking this course of action are far greater than the risk of actually doing so. You need decent housing, your family needs it, countless others are desperate for it, and society at large will reap the rewards.

TAKE ACTION AND REALIZE YOUR DREAM

I'm calling upon you, the reader, the new homeowner, the existing homeowner, our future developers, and providers of housing, to take action. Think differently, embrace the shared economy, subdivide an existing house for both you and your tenants, and help everyone out of this crisis in the process.

Being this person makes you an independent thinker who relies less on others and more on themselves for drive and ideas. It will gain you followers who will help you achieve those dreams.

WHERE DOES HOUSING COME FROM?

Our first family rental home, the one I lived in just after our family immigrated, didn't materialize out of thin air. Someone with vision and a keen sense of purpose had built those homes knowing that they provided an essential component of society's well-being. My family is a personal testament to that.

True, there was a business component to this as well. Those entrepreneurs saw an opportunity and ran with it. What I'm saying to you now is: *there exists, within the housing market, an opportunity for you (and existing homeowners) to take advantage of the current market to also earn an income.*

DECIDE YOUR LIFE NEEDS AN UPGRADE

What I'm suggesting is that many of you already have the wherewithal to become contributors to easing the affordable housing crisis, while fulfilling your own financial and life goals. The basis of this process is that nothing begins, however trivial or earth shattering, without a thought. To do anything, you must dream it first. Without the thought of change and why it's needed, nothing will change. And it's abundantly clear, change must occur.

THAT THOUGHT IS: I CAN BUY A HOUSE IF I THINK DIFFERENTLY

I want you to think about why this process might interest you. How much could you benefit by buying a house-as-a-business? How much closer to financial freedom would you be if you didn't have to worry about housing or a stable income?

Mindset Is Key

The heart of this book is to introduce you to the mindset needed to buy your own home and to inspire you to do other great things in the for-profit or not-for-profit home sector. By doing this, not only will you be able to buy yourself a house, but you're also going to be able to help yourself to accomplish great things in the future while inspiring others to do the same. Thus, you will all contribute to lessening the housing crisis.

Part of what I want is to transfer a degree of confidence that this has a very high likelihood of working. Historically, it has worked. Home ownership has been, and continues to be, one of the surest paths to financial freedom. Know that what I'm proposing is not fantasy, it's reality. It has been done, can be done, and will continue to be done over and over again. I want to assure you that you can do it too if you leave the traditional mindset behind.

> ***"No problem can be solved from the same level of consciousness that created it."***
> ***– Albert Einstein***

The above quote brings up two major points: *one*, we must understand the problem and *two*, we must divest ourselves of the outdated thinking process, or mindset, which got us here. The current situation, as I see it, is that the reality of new home ownership is challenging, to say the least. To put it bluntly, for those aspiring to own a home for the first time, home ownership has the appearance of slipping (or has already slipped) from their grasp.

Push

My entrance into the housing market didn't come because it landed on my lap, or that I understood the basics of the housing market, or that I knew how to find a decent place to rent. It came because I decided to "*push*" the rules a bit. Pushing did not mean flagrantly working outside regulations, it meant pushing the boundaries of existing rules so that they worked to my advantage, and to the goals that I'd set out for myself.

More importantly, I was pushing myself, my expectations, and my needs by entering the housing market in a way that was fundamentally different from what was traditionally done, yet still fulfilled my goals: financial and housing stability. In essence, I was willing to take what was available to buy, find the opportunities, and mold those opportunities to my needs. The truth about the current housing situation is not that it's unfair or stacked against you, it simply is that it's different from what your parents experienced.

I admit, I was at odds with the then-current thinking. But I was impatient. I wasn't willing to wait for everything to fall into place. I'd still be waiting if that were the case. On top of that, not acting meant that the feelings of hopelessness and despair would forever haunt me. I was having none of that. What I'm suggesting is that you shouldn't wait either.

> ***Because of my impatience and willingness to push, I was able to participate in a housing market where, had I applied traditional methods, I would have been unable to do so as quickly.***

In those first few years, I occupied the basement (the least desirable unit as far as collectable rents were concerned) and collected the higher rents from the two more desirable flats above. I'm telling you all this because what I'm proposing is not a theory. It is possible because I have done it. And as I've said before, what was groundbreaking was not that I had done it, was not that it was possible to do (anyone in my situation was free to take advantage as well), but that I had stepped outside the limits of my own expectations and comfort zone to creatively solve the challenges in order to successfully meet my life goals.

Your Vision Is Your Guide

You're already creative by nature—that's the way you were created. You have an extraordinary imagination, and you have great skills. Utilize your innate and learned skills and find people who have different skills to fill in the missing elements.

When I began converting my new house into a triplex, I didn't have the skills needed, but a friend of mine did. So, I brought him in to help me. He knew exactly what to do and I paid him to do it.

SKILLS CAN BE OBTAINED—WHAT YOU ABSOLUTELY NEED IS VISION

Without the vision, nothing can happen. In my case, I'd grown tired of the lack of privacy as a roommate and the fact that I didn't want to face rental payments for the rest of my life, or worse, expose my wife and children to that environment. I wanted something of my own. This consumed me. It was something that I saw from the future that made my present so very energizing. And I pursued this with vigor.

IT CHANGED EVERYTHING

This vision I had of my future inspired me into action. Sure, I could have coasted, but I soon realized that would be, at best, stagnation. So I allowed my vision to be my guide, to inform me of my short-, medium-, and longer-term goals. I can't begin to tell you how much that helped me—it changed everything.

Your Personal Action Plan

Take some time to think about, then commit to paper (or electronic form) an action plan that takes you from where you are now to where you want to be, be it five, ten, or twenty-five years down the road.

Understanding your 'why' is about starting fresh and deciding on one goal or dream that, when achieved, will mean a transformational change for your life.

There are two purposes to building this kind of plan:

1. **It forces you to think about how you see your life going forward.** Many of us don't have a clue where we're going, trusting conventional thinking and what comes our way. You need to know what makes you tick and what happiness and fulfillment looks like to you. Without that, you're making decisions in the dark.

2. **It keeps you on track.** Now that you know *where* and *how* you're moving forward, you can establish milestones and short-term and longer-term goals. This allows you to make course changes when changing conditions reveal new and exciting opportunities.

Once you've created this action plan, you can insert the opportunity to invest in a house-as-a-business and create a detailed business plan to minimize your risks.

Adapt to Succeed

An adaptable mindset is the secret to success. If you're resilient, you possess the ability to recover from a mistake or setback. We all aim to be resilient—but it's not enough. However, by being adaptable, you not only recover, but move forward into another phase of your development.

Adaptability assumes you've looked ahead, planned, and have given yourself options that enable you to change course as needed. Adaptability is the one key power that successful people have in spades. This is what keeps them, not only afloat, but leading in the race.

Buying a house-as-a-business requires adaptability. Conditions do change. New laws are enacted, market conditions vary, and tenants move out. By having a sound action plan and business plan, you're building adaptability into your life. This ensures stability and long-term financial success.

TheSelfFundingHouse.com

You will find planning tools here too!

As a bonus, you're part of a solution to solve an existential problem that nobody has solved, thus transforming the housing shortage worldwide. It's the right thing to do!

So, What's Next?

Since the early 1900s, the process of buying a house has essentially remained the same. But it's a different story now. Don't get me wrong, it's still done this way, but those sales are built upon the shoulders of existing equity from houses bought previously. Those entering the market for the first time either need financial help, creativity and vision, or a combination of both.

But I don't want you to get caught up with thoughts that home ownership is impossible. On the surface, it may look that way, but the real problem is that you have doubts.

> *"Doubt kills more dreams than failure ever will."*
> *– Suzy Kassem*

It's true that inaction condemns you to a life of perpetual renting. This may be fine for some, but for many of you, this does not work. As you see yourself progressing through your chosen career and thinking about having a family, do you want to continue to rent or would you rather own your own home? The answer is to jump in now, using the creativity you possess paired with a strong vision of becoming a homeowner.

Reframe how you see yourself and how you see the housing market. Remember, you're not alone in this situation. You do have skills, creativity, and drive as allies. Define your vision for the future and let that be the guide to your action plan.

The action plan serves another, deeper purpose: *it serves to help sell yourself to yourself.* You need a pep talk—and the best and most meaningful one comes from within. When that rush of adrenalin hits you, you'll know that what you've dreamed about can now become reality—nothing is going to stop you from getting there.

Decide your life needs an upgrade. Turn the obstacles to home ownership into opportunities. I have proven, and so have many others, that home ownership for someone on a modest income is possible if you're willing to commit to your dream of building a business as part of home ownership.

THIS IS NEXT

With a clear vision and a sound action plan, you can become part of a new generation of entrepreneurs on the way to multi-generational wealth and success. The economy will also benefit, and so will housing availability. It's a win all around.

2

Your Own Vision—Your Own Mindset

"Your vision is gold."
– Derek Lobo

Introduction

Likely, when you were a teen, you dreamed of someday owning a house. But you saw this happening in the same way your parents had done it. Suddenly, the current reality has shaken those dreams. And now you're looking around to see who's at fault and who can step in to restore the former reality. The truth is: *no one can ... except you!*

The place from which to restore that dream is *within*. Your parents worked within a mindset that benefitted them. Why would they try anything else if the process worked? You've got a different reality to work from, so you need to rethink what you already know and how you think about finding a solution that works today.

MINDSET OVERCOMES THE HOUSING CHALLENGE

What I'm proposing is that, with a mindset that takes today's housing market into consideration, instead of depending on your parents' mindset, you can enter into the housing market. Along with a clear action and business plan, you can begin to grow a business portfolio that will support your growing family and financial goals while also lessening the supply shortage. Buying a house-as-a-business is the answer—something only a few from our parents' generation have achieved, with as much purpose as I'm suggesting.

Yes, Things Have Changed

Before now, the method of financing a house remained essentially unchanged for decades. That is no longer the case. Traditionally, a home would cost approximately three times a person's yearly income. Today, that same home would cost 10 or 15 times a person's yearly income.

By this point in the book, you should be beginning to realize that buying a home is possible, but your parents' generation wouldn't understand the method—their approach no longer makes sense. Just like with new music, sometimes the older generation doesn't *get it*, but you do!

However, some things have improved. Today, interest rates are far lower than they have been in the past. We're no longer seeing double-digit interest rates (up to nearly 20%).

Some Things Have Not Changed

Whatever the end goal, your dream of home ownership is still the same as your parents'. You still crave the pride and independence of home ownership. But don't be too critical of older generations; the innate creativity of your parents was as strong as anyone's today. But instead of focusing that energy into purchasing a home, they could channel it into building a career or starting a new business. Buying a home didn't require creative thinking—the process was set.

CREATIVITY AND DREAMS ARE AS STRONG AS EVER

As a new buyer, your creativity and skills should now be channeled into buying a home-as-a-business. The end result will be the same—you'll begin to stabilize your financial situation, and at the same time give yourself a safe and secure place to live. It's not so much a radical departure from your parents' thinking, but a reframing of the focus into another area of living.

Expand Your Limits

It's inherently difficult to push back the assumptions you've grown up with and replace them with something altogether different. No matter where you turn, the advice seems to be the same. And to a great degree, many still think the only mindset available is the traditional one. But it doesn't have to be, and it shouldn't be. The current reality of home-buying dictates that you formulate something that works instead of trying to shoehorn old thinking into a vastly different reality.

> *A new mindset is vital for the successful execution of a new broad-in-scope goal —like buying your first home.*

Thousands of thoughts fly through your mind each day. Unfortunately, many of them are negative. They are beliefs about what you think you *can't do, shouldn't do*, or are conditioned *not to do*. There is an alternative—one that's always been available but has escaped mainstream thinking.

LET'S BRING THIS NEW MINDSET MAINSTREAM

Forget what your parents have done. You can't go there. I know that when you consider buying a house-as-a-business, the reality of home ownership becomes far clearer because the way a business is built remains the same as it has always been. See the next chapter, *Buying a House is Like Starting a Business*, for more on that.

I want you to think of this: *we tend to imagine living in a home that's a single-family unit—not an apartment, not a townhouse, and not one with a rented basement apartment or an upstairs flat.* We all tend to think of a single-family home. But the reality of housing is that a huge percentage of the population lives in multi-unit dwellings. And many of us have, at one time or another, been renters. The popularity of the single-family home is only partially explained by choice. Government incentives, zoning, media, advertising, and the housing industry all play a role in making the single-family home the de facto housing type. It doesn't have to be.

We Live Differently

Traditionally, you went to school, found a job, got married, your spouse had a job, you bought a house, paid the mortgage, and in 25 years, you owned that house. That was it. Simple.

Today, that entire process, or formula, has changed. Marriage often comes later in life, children even later, and schooling is not the panacea it once was. A three- or four-year university degree is not worth what it used to be. Today, you may consider taking specific courses that give you the knowledge you need, such as professional designations in real estate, insurance, technical training, mechanics, or some other field. In the past, fresh out of university, you found a job, be it for a business of some sort, became a teacher, worked in some level of government, or found a career in health care.

Living Arrangements of 25-34 Year-Olds

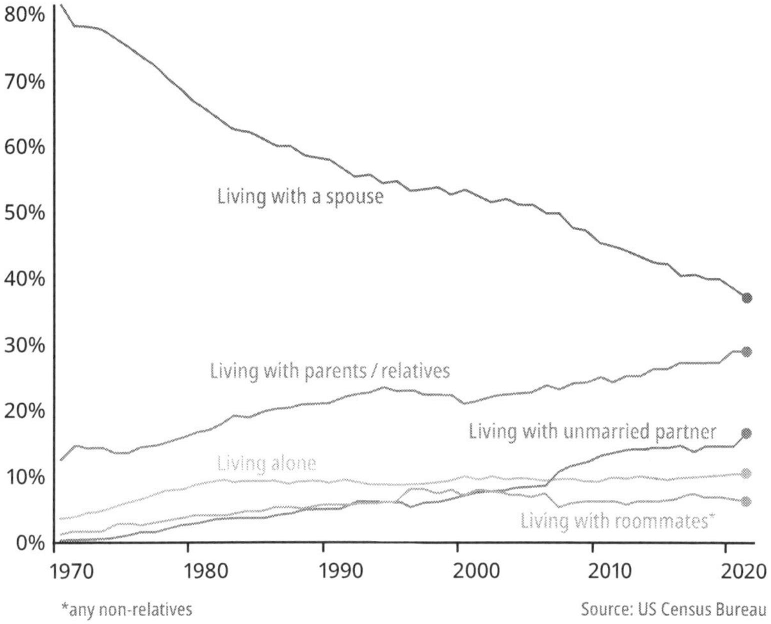

How Living Arrangements Have Changed Since the 1970s

But career choices have greatly expanded since the time of our parents. The choices are varied and numerous. Even the workplace has shifted, many working from home (a good work-from-home space further adds value to a house). So, it stands to reason that limiting yourself to the traditional ways of buying a home is illogical. Clearly, the old way is not working. And just as clearly, you must develop new ways that do work.

Once you are in the housing market, further increases in housing prices only ADDS value to your asset.

Equality of Opportunity

The housing situation, as it exists today, likely leaves your parents without an answer to your problem. Most parents are not able to buy their children a home. They may tell you to keep living at home and save more money. That's noble of them, but this may be only part of the solution. Maybe the solution should be to stay at home to save money, then buy a home and rent it out fully. That gives you entry into the market and begins building equity. That's a change in mindset.

> *In our world, we don't have equality of outcome.*
> *What we have is equality of opportunity.*

Not everyone gets to be a doctor. Not everyone becomes a professional athlete. Not everyone becomes wealthy by capitalizing on the latest trend. But if you're smart enough and creative enough with a solid vision, the government will lend you enough money to become a doctor. If you're financially well off, you can still become a doctor, but without the debt.

I want you, the potential house buyer, to look back upon your life to see what you've already achieved. I want you to give yourself credit for those *wins*. Remember, what you've accomplished is in *today's* economy, not that of the *past*—it's valid, valuable experience. What I see, to the credit of today's generation, is that you are *more* practical, *more* creative, and *more* resourceful than previous generations—because you have to be. Necessity is the mother of invention.

IF YOU REALLY WANT SOMETHING, YOU'LL FIND A WAY TO GET IT

In your parents' day, what the previous generation did was simply good enough. It got them the house they needed—they didn't have to do more. Now, we need that extra creativity to get to the same place. All the skills you've learned (that previous generations may not have had at the same age) can be applied to buying a house.

You, however, are much more collaborative by nature. Therefore, collaborative living is not an unrealistic option. It's practical and necessary. For example, co-living. There's nothing wrong with you being the superintendent of a house where others live with you and pay you rent. And what if the house has other services that can be monetized?

A quick note: I'm not advocating buying a house with your best buddy or with a group of friends—that's potentially a poor idea. Financing and buying a home with brothers and sisters, aunts and uncles, family, is likely a better alternative and may be a workable solution in your case.

TheSelfFundingHouse.com

Many resources such as sample partnership agreements and more!

The Lifetime House

By taking advantage of the current trends, by realizing that buying a house-as-a-business (thus having multiple sources of income) enables you to buy your forever home if you choose to do so. This is an important consideration. Additional rental income allows you to buy a larger house. As needs change, you and your family can take over more of the house. Later, your requirements may diminish, you can downsize and re-rent unused space.

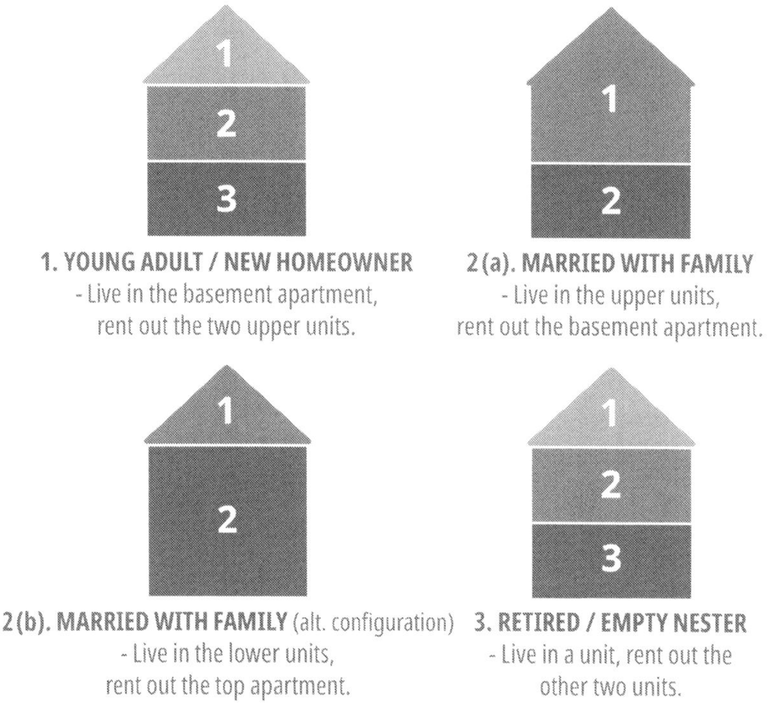

Examples of the use of a triplex over the lifetime of the owner

The possibility of buying a lifetime house is very real. This is a major shift from previous generations, who purchased their first house, then went on to their second, and third, and even further!

ADUs are becoming much more practical due to innovative methods of construction, making them cheaper and kinder to the environment. In addition, many existing homes can be altered to add safe and private additional living spaces. These homes are ripe to buy, waiting for the enterprising individual who sees buying a house-as-a-business as their path to financial freedom.

Hone Your Vision

An adaptable mindset is vital for successfully taking on a challenge as broad as buying your first home. What you need most is a clearly defined goal. If you don't have a goal to reach, getting there is difficult. All you see is where you've been (or are); the future is murky at best.

BEGIN WITH YOUR VISION

Your vision is gold. What do you want to do in terms of housing and financial freedom? With a clearly defined goal, it becomes far easier to go forward than trying to reach at something vague in the distance.

One of the things I did to bring myself back from a serious health scare was to put up pictures of buff rock stars in my exercise room—I wanted to look like them. Then I worked myself in that direction. And yes, I know the reality of me actually getting to look like them is a bit comical, but it helped me keep going—which was my real goal.

In the same vein, when a seasoned developer dreams up a new development that they would like to build, the first thing they do is hire an architect to draft a sketch or model of the plan. Sure, that's for advertising and selling the concept to politicians, etc., but it also puts that dream into a more concrete form so they can see what they're striving for, as well as doing the same for everyone else. With an excitement growing within you, serious work can begin on taking the project from concept to reality.

Take the time to hone your own vision of your future so that the vagueness gives way to clear and concise objectives. Write it down and keep modifying that vision until it feels right and feels like the real you. Trust me, doing this will make a huge difference. With that vision, a step-by-step plan (action plan) can be created to both clarify what you must focus on next *and* to keep you on track. These two things alone will lift much of your anxiety.

It's a New World—Embrace It

Prior to World War I, co-living was common and accepted. With the after-baby-boomer focus (post World War II) on single-family homes, that changed. But the sheer number of single-family homes takes a toll on the planet's resources. They cost more to build, heat, and drive the price of entry into the market too high. It's time for a reset of sorts, where multiple units in the same house come to be the norm again.

Some aspects of this new economy are actually beneficial. Interest rates are far lower, we have a much greater pool of ready information, social media keeps us connected, and our career choices have expanded exponentially. In short, the opportunities available to you are far greater than what your parents ever experienced.

Give yourself credit for your accomplishments. Focus on what is possible, as opposed to what you don't have. Use all the tools you now have available. This will clear the frustrations of inequality and free you to build on your own ideas and plans to further your goals and see your vision through.

Go and buy a house *and* a business and live your dream!

3

Buying a House is Like Starting a Business

"There are only two mistakes one can make along the road to truth; not going all the way, and not starting."
– Buddha

Introduction

If you've picked up this book, you're already interested in, not only buying a house, but buying one with a view to its purpose and management being business focused. This is a different focus than the traditional *buy and occupy the whole house,* then after some years, sell it for a bigger house or one in a better location.

It's likely the case that you don't have the needed down payment, and no matter how long you save, you're never going to accumulate enough. The reality is that you may not have wealthy enough parents to provide you with a down payment without seriously compromising their own financial health.

But despair is not what you feel. That's not you. Deep down inside, you're thinking you can pull away from the traditional approach to home buying, open yourself to new ideas which enable you to consider buying a home where you may have previously thought this possibility did not exist.

Well, you're right, not only is there possibility, there's real opportunity.

If there's something I really want you to take to heart, it's the fact that *you can afford to buy a house*. And I want you to know that if you free your creative mind to think differently—think like a business person even if you're not inclined to be in business—home ownership is indeed possible. The business side is well known, straightforward, and not difficult to set up and administer. It's a totally doable scenario.

The Business of Buying a House

When I bought my first house, I had no idea how to build a business. I didn't know all the ins and outs of becoming a landlord, I didn't know how to apply the sweat equity needed to convert a single home into flats, and I didn't know how to find or manage tenants. But what I did know, and had learned at an early age, is that having the right attitude supersedes ability and skills. Those last two can be learned. Or, if needed, can be obtained by hiring or asking advice from the right people. But to drive all that forward, I had to be in the right frame of mind.

ONE ACTION, TWO RESULTS

Buying a home and beginning a business are two means to the same end—financial stability and security. They're both dreams we have—we all want to own a home of our own and we all want to do something that brings us enough income for financial freedom. So why not combine the two?

In many ways, owning a house is like owning a business. However, the traditional way—how our parents did it—lacked the income-generating component. But the home still needed maintenance, house expenses needed to be paid and accounted for, and appliances needed to be kept running—Just like the business side of running a house as a business.

> ***People aren't buying a house for the price; people are buying the mortgage payment they can afford. Having ADUs increases the amount of mortgage they can afford.***

To be clear, I do know that many of you don't want to be in business. Business is hard, eats up time, means taking risks, and making sacrifices. It requires a specific kind of individual that is more comfortable dealing with the public and making sure the business side of the endeavor is working smoothly. But you're bringing in needed income to make home ownership possible in the first place. So, the minimal extra time needed for taxes and paperwork is not that onerous. The biggest bonus for all this effort, is that you've stabilized your financial outlook, and secondly, this first house could be the beginning of a new career path.

Who Are the Developers?

The vast majority of today's major home developers, and those who were successful before them, all began by buying or building a house. Ask yourself this question: *what if you're part of a group of individuals that—instead of finding careers in pharmaceuticals, education, or management—finds a career (with huge potential) in real estate development?*

If even a small percentage of existing homes added an ADU, it would go a long way to alleviating the housing shortage we currently find ourselves in. What if, by buying a house yourself, you're part of a group of developers that in 10 or 20 years from now, will end up solving the housing problem? I want you to think about what it is you really want out of house buying. Is it just a place *to* sleep at night, or is it a place that *lets* you sleep at night?

With your expanded mindset, your primary focus is now to acquire some housing-as-a-business acumen since you have grasped the entrepreneurial mindset of starting a home buying business. With that mindset, you could become the next Jeff Bezos or Elon Musk of the housing world. If either of those two had built houses instead of commodity sales and electric cars, we would not have a housing crisis today.

My Approach

What I did was this: *I took what was a single home and converted it into flats (two flats plus a basement flat, in my case).* That arrangement meant that I could live in one of the units and rent out the others, providing me with a source of revenue and providing the renters with housing that wasn't previously available.

The reality of my income was that I could not afford to support the whole house on my own—the rents generated were vital to the enterprise's survival. In essence, I had taken a business approach to my living needs instead of doing what many expect to do now (buy a home outright and occupy the whole structure).

I know that this process was not the first time it had ever been done, but it wasn't mainstream. I was at a point in my life that it made sense to me. What I'm telling you, the reader, is that many of you will feel that you're at the same point, thus able to quickly jump into this approach.

The Process

A short aside: when my wife and I were looking for our second house, I would always look at the basements first. After awhile, she asked, *"Why are you always running down to the basement?"* I think she was a bit annoyed. Why not first go look at what she was interested in? Our real estate agent, listening in, was also curious about my fascination with basements. I told them that I was thinking of putting in an office and/or rental unit down there. The agent shifted their approach and began showing us houses that made more sense to us. Really, I should have voiced my needs sooner—my mistake. Once the agent knew what was really needed, they soon found something I was interested in—since they knew where I'd spend my money.

Now, just because you haven't done it before, doesn't mean buying a house-as-a-business can't be done. Mostly, it requires you to design a process, to ensure everything gets done in a timely manner. The process then guides you. There's plenty of expertise available for the things you don't yet know. What you must do is get acquainted with this process from those who know how the financial/management side of buying the house and becoming a landlord work.

TheSelfFundingHouse.com

The Online Learning Portal assembles the knowledge, wisdom, and tools from many industry experts—making it easier for you to create your **Self Funding House™**

YOUR PATH TO HOME OWNERSHIP IS THROUGH BUILDING, CONVERTING, AND ADDING TO EXISTING HOMES.

There is a clearly defined path to do this. It is not a radical solution to an unsolvable problem. Buying a home is doable if you wrap your mind around the challenges and see things for what they are. Some are already buying houses in the way I'm suggesting. My hope is to make this process mainstream, with you as part of a new wave of business homeowners, thus alleviating the housing shortage.

Before I go on, this is not the story of buying a home where many families, and/or generations live together at the same time. Though viable for some, this is not the business model I'm proposing.

An Active Income Source

I'm not going to tell you that entering into home ownership in this way is easy. It does require some effort. It requires courage and creativity. But it does get you there. And it does result in the rewards that home ownership brings. In addition to those rewards, it gets you into the business side of home ownership, and the possibility of a much larger reward if extended to more housing and potential development on a grand scale.

> *"All the bad things that happen to you are the raw materials for future growth."*
> *– Dan Sullivan*

This is a change of perspective relative to the traditional path to home ownership. While your parents saw it as buying a place to live in, and the long-term growth as the value of the house increases, you'll see it as a place to live, plus, a place that generates a continuous source of income and the long-term growth in the value of the house.

Your Action Plan

The reality of life is *just doing it*. Nike is not wrong. *Doing it* does work for the simple reason that: if you don't do anything, nothing progresses. Life remains stagnant. Or, in light of the fast-paced life we live in, you're receding.

The link between that dream you have and the *doing it*, is the action plan (which includes the business plan). When you're actually doing something, you're moving forward in an organized and calculated manner. Executing that plan gets you closer and closer to that security and stress-free zone you've been dreaming of.

IT COSTS YOU $0 TO PUT IN AN OFFER

First rule: establish the geographic footprint you're willing to work within. Define that well. Then define what factors are important to you: transit, university/hospital proximity, development, highway access, etc. Finally, define the ideal house. Once that's firm in your mind, walking into the perfect house will evoke an immediate positive response. This is it! This is the one! It takes very little time to decide once the criteria is well established in your mind. At that point, the price becomes secondary (within your acceptable range) because you just know it will work as you intended and that dream you've had all along...will have come to life.

What you've done is you've figured out something that other buyers generally have not. For example, if the basement had a nine-foot ceiling, you know it's so much more valuable than one with an eight-foot ceiling (nine-foot ceilings make rooms feel more spacious). Local realtors and landlords can help you work through other factors that need to be taken into consideration.

Start making weekends your time to search for suitable houses. What you're looking for is a house that meets the criteria you've set out in the business plan. Just drive by all the others. The ones that you'll focus on, are those that give you the ability to put in an ADU (or two or three) and provide the necessary infrastructure to see your plan through.

Your Business Plan

To help you with developing your own business plan, I'm providing a checklist tool for starting the process. This will also serve as a sample of what's in store for you when you join The Self Funding House™ online learning portal.

Your FREE *Business Plan Checklist* is available for you to download now!

1. Go to TheSelfFundingHouse.com
2. Register for the FREE Dreamer Membership
3. Go to *Business Plan Checklist for Your Self Funding House™*
4. Download the checklist

This checklist is the starting point for your written business plan. Write everything down; don't rely on keeping it in your head. Your goal is to begin filling in the details needed to transition your vision of a Self Funding House™ from a dream to reality. The checklist is an opportunity to remind yourself of both the process as a whole and where more effort is needed. Ultimately, it leads to what's most important: *putting offers on houses that fit your business plan as you advance towards your long-term objectives.*

Plan to Reward Yourself

Businesses are not born of instant gratification. They are usually created with a written plan.

- Sometimes this plan is not followed exactly, but it is a solid guide.
- Have conversations with business owners about their business. You'll feel their pride and enthusiasm about what they have accomplished, or what they're planning to do. Their enthusiasm is contagious.
- Market knowledge is critical in real estate. No two houses are ever the same. The ability to spot a bargain and move quickly only comes with knowledge and experience.

The price paid for a house is not the most important factor. The most important factor is 'What can be done with that house' according to the business plan.

THE REWARDS

What impact will this have on you?

- You've shifted your mindset from 'Buying a House' to 'Starting a Home Ownership Business.'
- You've embraced the opportunity to take pride in selling yourself first, then expanding your resources to various investors and peers in order to increase equity and investments in your business.
- The foundation of your financial future will begin with the success of your 'Home Ownership Business.'
- This is the beginning of your new life. You've taken charge of your life and begun a business. This is going to impact many other factors and many aspects of your life going forward.
- The skills you've gained are transferable to other aspects of your life.
- You've created a step-by-step guide to help you navigate an uncertain future, ensuring success and wealth along the way.

Your Business Is Valuable

I want readers to realize that a house that's the basis of a business will be more valuable to the next buyer, thus increasing your gain there too. Not to mention, you're helping to solve the housing shortage/affordability problem.

My first home, and everything that went into its purchase, from my dream, collecting an income, paying taxes on the income, to knowing the capital gains were working in my favor, taught me some valuable lessons. To this day, I've not forgotten those.

With a young family on the way, we moved up one floor and rented out the basement instead. We had the room we needed and still collected most of the income. When our second child arrived, we took over the upstairs apartment. Some conversion of the existing layout was needed—such as changing the former kitchen into a nursery—to make it more of a single-family home. *Which, by the way, was what it was first built as.* The inner joke in our family is that we conceived a child on every floor.

That house allowed me to enter the housing market as a single guy, then allowed me to bring in a spouse, then grow a family. Later, when I started my own business, part of the basement became my office with room left over for a basement apartment, with its own outside entrance.

The house had now come full circle. Assuming I continued to live in that house, I could have converted that house into three apartments again—in stages if needed. Or, I could have housed my children in one of the units.

In essence, much of what you do when buying a home for yourself is like opening a business. The transition for buying a home in the traditional way and buying one with a focus on it becoming a business is completely doable and within the reach of anyone.

I'm here to assure you that buying opportunities do exist if you're willing to explore what's possible and dive into a method of thinking and framing challenges that overcome traditional biases.

BUSINESSES TRADE AT A PREMIUM BECAUSE OF THEIR REPEATABLE INCOME

Your potential rewards are huge. It all begins with your action plan, then progresses to a sound business plan—because you're not just buying a house, you're buying a business too. You're going to own a money machine. The repeatable income has a multiplier effect and creates more value than just the rental income. If and when the house is sold, you're not just selling a house—you're selling a business!

4

Business Requires Risk

"The biggest risk is not taking any risk. In a world that is changing really quickly, the only strategy that is guaranteed to fail is not taking risks."
– Mark Zuckerberg

Is There a Risk?

I want to make three points here:

1. Every business involves taking risks and collecting an income.
2. There is no business if you do not bring in revenue.
3. The right mindset is the key for success.

I agree that nothing is gained without taking some risks. But here, I'm talking about taking calculated, measured risks. This is where your business plan comes in. A good business plan is designed to mitigate the risks you'll take and give you an opportunity to explore your options.

Think back to the things you've accomplished and the risks you've already taken in life. You already have basic knowledge of how to minimize risks. Think of who you're dating, your first job, the courses you picked at school, and where you decided to work. They all involve taking risks. Give yourself some credit for what you've already accomplished, how you've handled it, and what you've learned from it.

In most businesses there is uncertainty about expenses and income. In a 'Home Ownership Business', there is certainty about the largest expense (the mortgage) and there is slightly less certainty about the operating costs for the house. But there is reasonable certainty around the income because market research has been completed and there is an understanding of demand. At worst, there could be a temporary reduction in rent (a tenant could move).

Identify the Source of the Risk

It's essential to know how you manage the risks you take. Some may see buying a house as a risk based on the opinions of another person, or sampling of others. What others say means a lot and has sway in how you'll proceed. However, you're basing a decision you'll be accountable for on others (who aren't accountable). This usually means you've not fully bought into your own strengths and abilities.

Still, others may decide that following rules, guidelines, or accepted behavior is the way to go. True, following rules is good. It's better than relying on the opinions of others whose mindset may be mired in the past, or simply too afraid to tell you what they truly think. But following guidelines, policies, and accepted behavior, is not an effective risk management strategy. Those guidelines are born from an older system of belief. Accepted behavior means you don't have a good grasp of the available information and therefore cannot process it intelligently.

To do that, you must be aware of all the information you can lay your hands on, filter that data against how you want to achieve your goals, what the risks are at your stage of life, and accept that the decisions you make are yours and yours alone, and the failures are yours too. This does not mean you don't seek advice or fail to adhere to the rules. It means you take those into account but base the risk on criteria you've set for yourself. It's taking ownership of the situation, doing due diligence, creating an action plan, and making it work for you.

HISTORICALLY, CALCULATED RISKS PAN OUT

A calculated risk is different from following the crowd or simply falling in step with the normal way of doing things—it's being creative and pushing the system to get what you need. And if that need is home ownership, then with a good action/business plan and some education, you'll soon be a home and business owner.

Those who have done what I have done—buy a house-as-a-business—are not followers, nor are they conservative in their thinking. They're motivated individuals who see the value of home ownership and know the risks associated with owning a house-as-a-business are calculated, but supported by historical data.

Perceived vs. Real Risk

We have a natural urge to protect ourselves from real and perceived threats. There are real threats to deal with, but we often spend much more time worrying about perceived threats than reality calls for. We have a hard time knowing how to differentiate a perceived threat from a real one.

When our very existence is threatened, the anxiety it generates is warranted. We need to be aware of these threats. We also need a way to figure out when a threat is triggered by a lack of knowledge.

If you've done your homework and you've decided that buying a house-as-a-business makes sense to you, don't let someone else drive up your anxiety by telling you it can't be done. Trust your own instincts, your skills, and your action/business plan. They measure the real risks—that's what they were designed for.

Your Achievements Add Up

As a younger person, you've already achieved many things, some of which you might not have thought you would, despite how you may feel and what expectations were placed upon you. You're educated, have a job, and probably have great computer skills (far better than most of the older generation). Therefore, there has been significant growth in your life already. So don't let this current housing scenario overshadow what you've done.

Life isn't over just because you think you can't participate in the housing market. It's merely another challenge—really, you've already navigated more complex issues. Realize that a large part of the fear of buying a first home is the lack of knowledge—it's all new to you. But it isn't new for those who've done it before. You merely have to think of buying your first home like it's buying your second home, except you've enlisted professionals to do some of the nitty-gritty with you.

TRUST YOUR BUSINESS PLAN

With a business plan, your risk will be significantly reduced. Even if you put in an offer and it's rejected, nothing terrible happens—you simply try again. The rest is merely going through well-defined steps. It's not the daunting task some make it out to be—it's simply a process.

Buying a house is not the biggest decision you'll ever make. The bigger decisions are typically *deciding on a career path* and *finding a partner that will be with you for the rest of your life.* Those decisions are very tough to unravel. Years of training or university can never be recovered. Changing careers is arduous and time consuming. And the dissolution of a romantic partnership is painful.

In contrast, with a well-thought-out business plan, buying a house that will generate income is much less risky because the house typically retains its value and the incomes generated will keep coming. Even buying the wrong house is fixable by selling it back with minimal loss. You gain some knowledge and try again.

Perspective Is Everything

Put the risk in perspective! In the case of housing, it is a short-term risk. This is likely a good bet. The first five years may be a bit uneven (as in any business), but as time moves on, the rewards start compounding.

The first step is easy: *dream about it.* Have the courage to dream. Give yourself permission to dream and not feel it's a waste of time—it's certainly not! Bring that dream front and center, so you can feel its power. That gives you a goal.

I DREAMED OF OWNING A HOUSE, SO I PURSUED THAT DREAM

Take a moment to visualize your future. Where will you be in 10 or 15 years? Where do you want to be? Sit down for a minute and write out a plan for your future. Then write out a set of actions (your action plan) that take you to that place. And while you're at it, build out a business plan for that triplex you should buy so you can house yourself at the expense of others (from the rent you'll charge).

Once this is in place, it's simply a matter of finding a professional who understands the steps, so your plan is executed properly. This part is all technical. No one is going to judge you or give you a grade. You're driving this. And you'll only fail if you don't try. Once the first house is purchased, the second, the third and fourth, are easy. And you can impart your knowledge to others to encourage them to do the same.

Embrace the opportunity to take a risk with the correct tools and knowledge. You don't need to buy the biggest most expensive house on the street.

What you must understand about this process is that the biggest hurdle is the mind shift. It's not the financing, the house hunting, or creating the business plan. Once your mind focuses on accomplishing this goal, you will get it done.

"When you've been bothered about something, think of what you'd be doing if you weren't bothered."
– Dan Sullivan

If you view this as an opportunity and not a problem, you can make some great strides.

The Risk of NOT Doing It

Given that many of you are relatively young, you likely don't have too much to lose. You may have a car, and even some savings, but most young people simply haven't had the time to accumulate much material wealth. Chances are that your children are very young or are still in your future. If you indeed buy a house and things go south, the house will not devalue. You can rest easy knowing that it is possible to recoup most, or all, of its value, leaving you in a similar situation where you were to begin with.

But if you decide to do nothing, you'll be stuck in an outdated framework of thinking. This will limit your possibility of seeing new options and will, ultimately, prevent you from purchasing a home and gaining the financial stability and freedom you so desire. We often don't think about how solid an investment a house is. It's not a commodity, like a car or anything you buy from a store. Traditionally, market prices have risen even after short periods of time.

BUYING A HOUSE IS NOT A HAIL MARY PASS

This is not how you would feel if you were 50 years old with an investment portfolio, dependents, and facing retirement in 15 years or less. At that point, you can't afford to risk everything—there's not enough time to recover. The damage could be catastrophic for you and your family.

But now, still young, the risk really is *how long do you wait?* And the short answer to that is: *don't wait*. Because the real risk is *not taking the risk* and never getting on the path to your dream of financial freedom. The ability to take some risk, whether it leads to success or failure, allows for more risks to be taken in the future.

Nothing ventured, nothing gained.
No risk, no reward. Stagnation.

Trust Your Business Plan

Having a sound business plan is your friend. Having multiple sources of income is your friend too. What if you had a house with a basement apartment, a top floor flat, and you lived on the main floor with a roommate (or two)? What if you rented the garage to a local band for practice space, remodeled it for an office rental, storage rental, or a workout area? You could even rent the excess driveway space to a neighbor, or rent that unused backyard to a gardener wanting to grow vegetables.

MONETIZE EVERYTHING

What I'm saying is: *monetize everything about your house.* When a flat becomes temporarily empty, or your roommate goes to Europe, you can Airbnb the space. The more you can monetize, the more sources of income you have, and the more secure your finances become.

I was okay with monetizing the more desirable two upper flats in the house I bought. The basement would have brought in less income, and as a single guy, I didn't need as much space anyway. By strategically assessing what you've bought (or intend to buy), you can fill in a few extra lines of your business plan in the plus column, even if it doesn't come to a big number like a unit rental would. But remember, those smaller items bring in cash month, after month, after month. It all adds up faster than you might think.

DIVERSIFY—HAVING MULTIPLE SOURCES OF INCOME IS BEST

With more sources of income, you've further decreased your risk and given yourself a good understanding of business, income, expenses, mortgages, write-offs, etc. These are great skills to have when planning to buy your second house or starting another business in the future.

The Upside Is Tremendous

We all know, deep down, that nothing really happens without some risk. Everything we do involves a degree of risk. Our focus, when considering home ownership, is to find out what the risks really are, how to manage them, and build them into our business plan. Those who have a post-secondary education have already taken a bigger financial risk than this. They invested their time and money into school, hoping it would lead to a highly focused career—which doesn't always happen.

Take a moment to assess the risks that apply to you, not those of the average person, but *the you* that's motivated and calculated enough to assess the risks involved in proper context. Then factor in the risks you've already taken, be it finding a job or applying for post-secondary education and taking on a student loan.

The uncertainty of starting a business is no greater, providing your business plan is sound. Buying a house-as-a-business is a more stable business than most, due to the primary asset's price stability and the high demand for that housing. So, even if everything deviates from your plan, what you lose is minimal. Remember, no one buys a house thinking it will lose value. The reason being: history has shown that housing is reliable and house prices trend upward over the long term. You're playing the long game.

Your Self Funding House™ has tax advantages too—expenses and mortgage interest become tax deductions, that a standard homeowner does not get!

Now, once you own a single house, the door is wide open for far greater rewards. Think of the developers that build all the housing lining the streets. The vast majority of them began their business by buying or building a single house. From there, they developed it into a highly successful business. That opportunity is still available to you and readily achievable. I encourage you to jump on it and seize your opportunity for financial freedom.

5

Foundation of Your Financial Future

"The only way for a young person to buy a house today is to become a landlord."
– Günther Bluesz

Introduction

How we approach decisions in life and what decisions we actually make usually boils down to a few basic needs: *who we partner with, what will be the path to financial stability,* and *where we live.* The remaining aspects of our lives, while important, are of lesser significance, and don't tend to affect our lives to such a high degree.

What I foresee, is that the path to financial freedom and to housing security will become one and the same for an increasing number of us. If we buy a house-as-a-business, we get both. If we decide to expand the number of units we rent out (via more houses), the business side can quickly grow into a career. If we decide to build our own rental units, we become developers.

BUYING YOUR FINANCIAL FREEDOM

Shifting your mindset about buying a house really boils down to how you are going to go about achieving your financial freedom. It's about your goals and your dreams. It's about security and financial success. And it's about your future.

Changing your mindset requires effort. Habits are not easy to break. The act of defining your mindset forces you to think about how you view the world. If you're this far into the book, you're likely well positioned to see housing as the potential foundation for your financial success. So, you're well on your way.

This is not so different from what's been traditionally done. Our parents bought a home and sat back to watch the equity grow as they pursued their careers. What I'm proposing is nearly the same, except the financing of your first home is structured differently, and the potential path to huge financial success is now available where it wasn't so easy for your parents. The impact of choosing to buy a house-as-a-business is profound and far reaching. In retrospect, owning a house that paid for itself was perhaps the most meaningful thing I've ever done in my business life. It gave me the confidence to pursue other business goals.

I PROVIDED MYSELF WITH OPTIONS, NOT DIRE PROSPECTS

Had I lost my job, I would still have had enough income to survive, keep my house, and have time to find another job, or perhaps buy another house where all the units were rented. The importance of buying that first house cannot be overstated. It made me financially secure from day one (because my collected rents exceeded expenses). You can do the same for yourself!

You Are Adaptable

There's nothing wrong with being a renter for the rest of your life. Though the home is an emotional buy, you can be happy living in an apartment as a great many do. Everyone has a different view of the world and we all have diverse ways for managing our needs and finances. We must make ourselves happy by whatever means we can. In Europe, renting is the norm. To many, it's what's expected, and many seem to do quite well living this way.

The problem is that by lacking that huge asset when nearing the later part of your life means you've got little to show for all those rental payments. For many of us, we need a home's value unlocked to survive. Sure, there are many other ways to invest your money, but the house is the most common way to secure financial freedom. For those whose interests lie elsewhere, do what you think will work for you. However, the basic building blocks for whatever you choose are the same: *a vision, creativity, a business plan, and an action plan*. But for many others, home ownership is their dream.

A HOUSE IS LIKELY THE SAFEST BEDROCK OF THEM ALL

To get to that dream, you'll need to create a financial bedrock you can depend on. It could be stocks, cryptocurrency, house ownership, or any other business that enables you to earn enough to gain financial freedom. Businesses go under, stocks fall, and cryptocurrencies are volatile. But housing is stable over the longer term. Rarely do housing prices fall precipitously. Remember, you cannot live in your Bitcoin, and you can't eat your stocks. Though owning a home is not the only viable solution, it is the most stable solution.

If owning a house-as-a-business is your goal, then this book (and those in the series that follow) combined with The Self Funding House™ Online Learning Portal are your roadmap forward.

Buying a house-as-a-business allows you pride of ownership, housing security, family security, and has historically been a great investment. For those of us who believe this, and are willing to adapt, this book is how you get into it.

The Numbers Prove Feasibility

If you assume that owning a house will mean working from paycheck to paycheck while barely making ends meet, you might want to take the time to run the numbers. When accounting for all the costs of buying a house, breaking down each item into an easily readable and logical format, it's easy to see how buying a house-as-a-business does indeed work—the numbers prove it.

Here's an example of a typical scenario:

FINANCIAL MODEL FOR: *Owner occupies main floor - basement unit rented*		
HOUSE PURCHASE	Total Purchase Price	**$500,000**
	Down Payment (%)	**20%**
	Down Payment	**$100,000**
	Renovation Budget - Basement ADU	**$75,000**
RENTAL INCOME	Rental Rate *(LOWER UNIT)*	**$1,500**
	Utilities Charged *(LOWER UNIT)*	**$56**
	Rental Income *(ANNUAL)*	**$18,672**
MORTGAGE & EXPENSES	Mortgage *(MONTHLY)* 5.5% Interest	**$2,271**
	Mortgage *(ANNUAL)*	**$27,254**
	Additional Expenses *(ANNUAL)*	**$13,031**
	TOTAL EXPENSES *(ANNUAL)*	**$40,285**
NET OPERATING INCOME*	NOI *(ANNUAL)*	**-$21,610**
	NOI *(MONTHLY)*	**-$1,801**
	Required Household Income**	**$72,033**

** NOI = (Net Operating Income) What you're paying to live in the house and own it*
*** Based on 30% of annual income for housing (guideline)*

- This is a simplified, basic model to illustrate the approximate income needed, the impact of your Self Funding House™ expenses, and what it will cost to own your Self Funding House™.
- These examples don't show all the details (moving expenses, living expense details, renovation costs, etc.) It is a demonstration of the basics.
- Many banks provide mortgage calculator tools online, which you can use to get an idea of your qualifications.
- Financial models for other purchase prices, and for renting upstairs units are in the appendix of this book.
- Additional detailed spreadsheets and instructions are available in TheSelfFundingHouse.com online learning portal (Entrepreneur Membership).

There is only so much detail I can go into here on these pages. The previous examples are general models for the purpose of understanding the basics. The great news is that we have a complete working model spreadsheet for you to download and use for creating your financial model. It's part of the *Entrepreneur Membership* in the SelfFundingHouse.com Online Learning Portal. There, you will also find complete instructions, videos, and examples for using this tool.

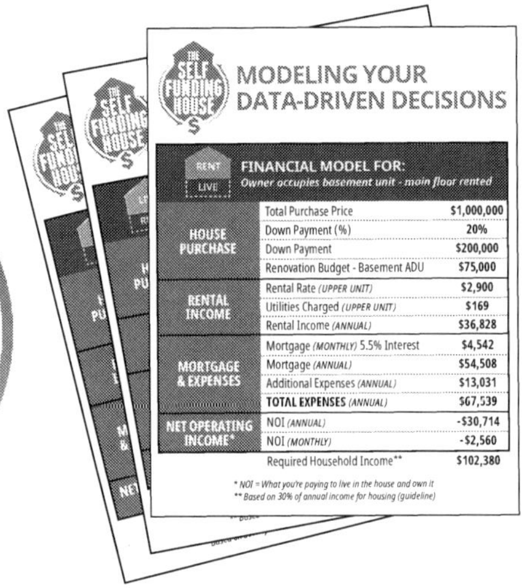

TheSelfFundingHouse.com
Sign-up for the Entrepreneur Membership to access
"The Financial Model for Your **Self Funding House™**"

Your responsibility is to get an understanding of the 'Home Ownership Business', create an action plan, and consult with those who have found success doing what you're planning to do. With some, or all, of the down payment saved, and creative strategies adopted to acquire the money you don't have (examples: approach investors or established family members to become business partners), you're on your way. Refer to the *Financial Solutions* section at the back of the book for some strategies.

THE BEGINNINGS OF A VIABLE, SUSTAINABLE, INCOME FOR LIFE

In a few years, the value of the house will appreciate, rents will slowly increase, and your mortgage principal will decrease. The equity in the house will also be higher. In less than 10 years, you may consider buying another house and renting out all the units, thus bringing in more income—enough to support the mortgage plus real income.

Capitalize on Your Mistakes

Buying my first house and turning it into a triplex was one of the best decisions I've ever made. It put me on a course of financial stability like nothing I'd ever done to date. I knew then, with rent coming in and the fear of unemployment banished, I had it made. Financial freedom. That feeling of elation is still with me. And to a great degree, it created my current career. But I did make one poor decision that I regret to this day.

After my family had grown and my business allowed me to leave my employment and be on my own, I decided to sell that house. At the moment, it seemed right. My wife and I felt we needed a single home so that's what we did. But it was a very poor business move. I should have kept the house for business reasons and sentimental reasons as well.

DON'T SQUANDER A SOURCE OF INCOME

Had I decided to buy a single home *and* keep the house we'd moved out of as a rental; I'd still have that income stream, and, with a few more houses, would have been able to greatly supplement my income. As it was, I let that opportunity slip by because, in that span of time, I'd forgotten that a self-supporting house needs no resources from me. I could have even hired a professional management company had I not wanted to be hands-on like I'd always been.

Selling that house was a mistake, and I don't want you making the same error in judgment. Buy one house, live in it, then as you want something different, keep the house that made everything possible and keep building on that momentum. The added income will flow for many years.

Build Your Foundation for Financial Stability

It's a proven historical fact that homeowners are more financially secure than non-homeowners. With the shared-economy concept taking hold, a high demand for affordable housing, an abundance of houses that could easily be converted to accommodate ADUs (basements, flats, backyard homes, etc.), and a creative generation of individuals who crave financial and housing stability, the opportunity for buying a house-as-a-business has become more than near reality—it's here now!

I know that at the time I bought my first house to convert into a triplex, I was firmly outside of the norm. Most people wanted a single-family home. The mindset of that generation had been set by decades of doing the same old thing. We've clearly moved beyond that mindset. Financial freedom can be achieved in far more diverse ways, and new opportunities arise every day. The buying-a-house-as-a-business opportunity is but one of many. However, it's one of the best because of its stability and demand.

By taking action now, you're building the foundations of a financial future that will free time, energy, and resources to concentrate on the other components of living a fulfilling life. After 25 years (or less), with no mortgage, the house becomes a stable revenue source. Incoming rent pays for all the house expenses and a great deal more. At this point, you've become financially bulletproof.

6

Living in a Shared Economy

"We used to live in a world where there were people, private citizens, a world where there are businesses, and now we're living in a world where people can become businesses in 60 seconds."
– Brian Chesky

Introduction

We've all heard about the shared economy, and we've all participated in it. It's everywhere, from the ride service we summon (Uber, Lyft), to the selling of merchandise, tool rentals, to professional services and healthcare.

The shared economy is not only about Uber, Airbnb, or your home ownership business—it's a concept that's expandable to many other areas of life and business.

I think we all sense that we're on the cusp of a burgeoning shared economy—it will be a large part of the world's future. We share a range of items, from luxury jets, to tools, cars, or houses—nearly anything is shareable. The economy is increasingly moving in that direction. You, as an owner of a house with ADUs, are part of that shared economy.

Shared Economy Defined

The shared economy can be viewed as a philosophy that strives to gain as much value as possible from existing assets for the benefit of both the owner of that asset, and for those who make use of it. It's more than just a means to an end for the owner, it benefits society at large. In a shared economy, assets are shared in a more collaborative way. In this way, physical assets become services instead of being used solely by the owner.

The shared economy is an extremely fast-growing part of our economy, attracting millions in venture capital and fast becoming the basis of many businesses. This is made possible due to advances in big data and online platforms. With online support, individuals and businesses can make the needed transactions quickly and easily. This allows the generation of income for individuals and businesses from the resources they own—such as a car, house, or construction tool.

The most obvious examples of a shared economy at work are the ride sharing services such as Lyft or Uber. An individual car owner can provide transportation services to the public-at-large through online connections (such as an app on a phone). It enables that person to use their car for income where, in the traditional economy, it would sit largely unused for most of the day. That owner can work part-time or full-time, depending on their goals, while paying for a car they couldn't normally afford or generating a full income.

Ride sharing isn't the only shared economy focus. The purchasing of goods via online companies (such as eBay) is widespread. New and used goods can be bought by any one person from any other person worldwide. To name a few: accountants, copywriters, appliance services, at-home health professionals also participate by offering freelance work.

Many other sectors will gradually shift to a shared economy approach in the coming years. For us, I'm going to focus on the shift to a shared housing economy.

Underutilized Assets

A shared economy enables individuals to monetize assets that are not fully utilized. In our case, we have thousands of houses that can be modified to accommodate ADUs where none currently exists. It highlights the ability—and perhaps the preference—of individuals to rent, rather than own them.

THINKING DIFFERENTLY FOR SOLVING CHALLENGES

Younger buyers think differently. Here's an example: for many years now, picking up a stranger in your car was something you wouldn't even contemplate. The perceived dangers far exceeded the potential good you'd do by giving that person a lift. But what about now, as you pull out your phone to call for an Uber?

Think about it, if you're driving for hire (Uber), you'll willingly go to a specific location and pick up an individual that you've never seen or even heard about and let them sit in your car until you drop them off. And you'll continue to do this, ride after ride, day after day. So, what has changed? That same change is the basis for allowing a tenant to share your home (such as a basement apartment) while you live in the main portion.

Note that Uber has accountability measures in place to ensure driver safety. Similarly, as a landlord, you'll vet your tenants properly to ensure your safety and privacy.

The Future of The Shared Economy

Strangely, we do not have a shortage of housing (though media coverage may lead you to think that way) in Canada. We have enough square footage for all of us to live in. One of the main drivers of the housing shortage is that we have countless thousands of big houses that are not subdivided, sitting on large lots.

HOW NEW CONSTRUCTION CAN FACILITATE FUTURE SHARING

There is enough housing supply, but it's configured poorly to ease the housing shortage. With a few thoughtful changes to new housing, the shortages would soon be a thing of the past. I've suggested, and many others have as well, that all new houses have an accessory unit roughed in and designed to make subdivision possible. By adding access to the basement, garage, backyard or laneway, and other safety considerations, adding an ADU becomes a matter of just doing it. After construction is completed, adding those features becomes far more difficult and expensive. A thoughtfully designed home thus becomes more valuable because options are available.

When designing and building an apartment building, anything that can augment the rental income creates more value for the owner, such as parking, laundry, storage, cell tower and cable, etc. There's no reason why you can't think of housing in the same way. The unused parking space in your double driveway could be rented out. Or the unused backyard has room for a detached small house. Every source of income brings you closer to easier affordability or shorter mortgage terms/lesser payments.

However, there are zoning issues. Some neighbors don't want rental units in their area and may object. The way to mitigate this is to have a clearly defined set of municipal rules for these situations. Then everyone knows what is possible and legal, and what is not. At this point, without valid objections, a house can be separated into apartments without issue.

MAKING ADUs THE NORM

Another avenue for more housing is unused office space. The work-from-home mentality has taken root and won't let up. There will always be a significant percentage of workers who prefer working from home, freeing former office space. Converting office towers to rental units is actually being done now. But it needs to go further and progress faster.

Take Advantage of the Shared Economy

There is a real shift going on. California has now legalized accessory housing units in the backyard. They've gone from 255 units five years ago to 19,000 units last year (2021). And they're building new housing with accessory housing units attached. The services are already built into the lot, all they're doing is adding a bit more space for a second unit. This is what a shared housing economy looks like.

None of this means your life gets worse. Smart design would make privacy and safety a priority, thus you'd never feel imposed upon or anxious because of noise or privacy. Design is everything. This contributes to your life, either via the added income or simply having good neighbors of your choosing as tenants. They may share in the chores or become your best friend. And they'll watch your home when you're away.

GET IN NOW

Where would you rather be, at the front of the curve or behind it? How many more things are going to get shared? What about the backyard pool you pay to maintain? Is it mostly unused? If your children have moved away, your pool is empty most of the time, making it available for rental (check out swimply.com).

What do you want to accomplish? What is your motivation? Have you written out your action plan? What do you want your financial outlook to be in 10 years? Where do you want to be living in 10 years? Can the shared economy concept drive your dream forward?

The shared economy creates a solution to one of society's more pressing problems—affordable house ownership and affordable rental housing. I can't stress enough the importance of getting in now. The shared economy is growing and will continue to grow. Get in on the ground floor and reap the rewards for the rest of your life.

This book, and the others to follow, are formalizing the process into a replicable plan. Housing prices will never be three times a person's income again. The housing market will never be the same as it once was. By buying a house-as-a-business now (instead of waiting forever), you're gaining access to a huge potential payoff—financial freedom—and helping to solve the housing crisis. *How much better could it be?*

Embrace the Concept

Every time I get into an Uber, I'm fascinated by the concept. Why does the driver do this? What is their favorite shift? How is it working for them? I remember my wife and I being picked up by a woman driver. She told us that it's so much safer for her to drive compared to a traditional taxi. She knows who she's picking up and where they're going. And she works when she wants to. For her, the shared economy has provided a reliable source of income.

Even though the shared economy has existed for an exceptionally long time (tool or car rental, for instance), recent years have seen an explosion of shared economy businesses come into being where previously none existed. Society has embraced the concept and understands how it works, participating without hesitation. And now the shared economy can be the foundation of your own house-buying strategy.

As for buying a house-as-a-business, I want you to understand that you can buy something like a multiplex and rent most of it out while occupying a unit yourself. Your mortgage is paid, you're bringing in a rental income, and your financial stability has improved considerably. You now have a clear path to an interesting and rewarding career.

By embracing the concept, it couldn't be better. I strongly urge you to join the shared economy trend and reap the rewards. You, and the world, will be far better off for it.

7

Knowledge Overcomes Fear

"Your wealth is hiding under the very thing you are afraid to do. It's time to face your fears and take action. Expect Miracles."
–Joe Vitale

Introduction

I suspect the potential of getting a bad tenant is the number one fear new landlords face. By bad, I mean those who don't pay rent, don't respect the privacy of others, or those who cause harm to either the dwelling or those living nearby. Reality does not support that fear.

Most of us have, at one time or another, been tenants. That means we've lived among other tenants. And I'll bet the worry about what those tenants might do, did not keep you up at night. If you speak to current landlords, bad tenants are not foremost on their minds. They've grown out of those worries long ago because experience has proven that the fear of bad tenants is largely unfounded.

LEARNING TO PUT FEAR IN ITS PLACE IS EMPOWERING

The second greatest fear potential landlords face is the same fear anyone feels when starting a new business—they're not sure what they *need to do, how to do it,* or *when.* Thirdly, they're not certain that they're up to the task of handling the responsibility associated with running a business. But ask any small landlord and they will tell you that, while there is some time that needs to be allocated to the business side of things, they'll also tell you that once the processes are ironed out, it's just a matter of going through the motions.

If business was so difficult, no one would be doing it. The reality of owning a business is that once the income begins rolling in, it's all good. Once you buy a house and the units are generating income (so your mortgage is getting paid), you'll soon relax into the fact that you actually own a home and it's paying for itself (and potentially more, in many cases).

You're Not Alone

For those thinking that being a landlord is tough, take a good look around. There are countless landlords, from all walks of life, all ages, in all stages of business acumen, making a successful go of it. It's been done as long as houses have existed. There are plenty of resources available to inform new landlords about the laws, maintenance, and the issues that come from renting units.

One of the most remarkable things in society is the power of the community—the ability to share information with like-minded individuals who have similar goals and targets as you do. That support helps solve problems, is a source of advice gained from experience, and provides encouragement when needed.

TheSelfFundingHouse.com
Learn about becoming a landlord and discover tips for success.

With ADUs becoming increasingly common, there will be a community of individuals in your exact position ready to support and supply the resources you need for successful and trouble-free ownership.

FEAR = False Expectations Appearing Real

> ***When renting an apartment, go and visit the prospective tenant in their current location.***

From that visit, you'll get an immediate sense of who they are and how they treat their space. Though it may feel like you're prying, this method, from experience, works. By completing reference checks and all the logical things a landlord should do before renting, you'll weed out those you don't want and find those that will respect your needs and your property. In general, people don't destroy what they rent. If you do proper advanced screening, proper financial checking, talk to references, and have clearly defined rules of conduct (with enforcement), the likelihood of disruptive behavior is rare. And don't forget that your own network of co-workers, friends, and family is often the best avenue for finding a suitable tenant.

If you're paralyzed by the fear of beginning a business or afraid to properly vet potential renters, then maybe this route to success is not the one for you. Remember, there are many roads to success.

Points to consider:

- Fear of owning a house: half the population owns a home. The process is very well understood and clearly defined. Questions can be answered quickly and easily. Though you may feel anxiety when purchasing your first home, you'll soon see the fear is unfounded, but the excitement lives on. You're just doing the same thing as everyone else.
- Fearing for your safety is unfounded. Millions of people live with close neighbors the world over—it's a business relationship (tenant-landlord).
- How many of you have rented something and left it in fine working order? Or returned cleaned tools? Or stayed at an Airbnb and left that place unblemished? Millions rent and leave the rented item in perfect shape.
- You've likely stayed at a bed and breakfast or hotel. How many times were you really worried about the person next door?

Case Studies

CASE ONE

The process an actual landlord uses to find tenants to live with (in their words):

1. I don't post on Kijiji or Craigslist (although I know some people who do). I've never found it necessary. My first step is to ask my close friends if they know anyone who needs to rent a room. If this doesn't turn up any good candidates, then I post that I have a room available on Facebook/Instagram. I always get more than enough responses from my social media to find an ideal candidate.
2. The vetting process is crucial. An in-person meeting is necessary to determine if the potential tenant is compatible to live with.

   Things to discuss in this meeting:

- Work/sleep schedules.
- Shared responsibilities around the house.
- Pets. (I have a cat. I will not rent to anyone with a pet because that would upset my cat. My tenants know they cannot bring pets into my home).
- Expectations of cleanliness in common places.
- Expectations regarding guest(s) in the house.
- Explanation of how utilities are split between housemates. (I split everything evenly with my tenants).
- Discussion about shared resources. (I have a band rehearsal space that I am comfortable sharing if people are respectful of my equipment and inform me of rehearsal times. I also have a veggie garden that I am comfortable sharing, if housemates contribute to its upkeep).

3. It is very important to have a written agreement between yourself and the tenant to ensure the rental terms are well understood and well documented. *NOTE: be sure to conform to local laws for landlords and tenants.*

CASE TWO

Kelly's perspective on being a tenant:

For a period of years, I was a tenant, renting one flat of a triplex. Another tenant lived below me while the landlord occupied the third unit. I remember those years quite fondly, as they were relatively carefree.

The relationships I had with my landlord and tenant were very positive. After a while, we all became friends. In my own mind, I was more than a tenant just renting an apartment, I had become part of the house, and was treated as part of the greater household by everyone. I knew my landlord's family and felt connected to them in a way that became more than a landlord-tenant relationship. And I became fast friends with the other tenant and his circle.

Because we all lived together, sort of, I knew what was going on, peripherally, in the whole house—as they did. I could choose to participate in their lives as much, or as little, as I wanted to. I really liked living there. It gave me options and a great sense of security and partnership.

At one point, the other tenant moved out, necessitating the landlord find a replacement. That would mean the dynamics of the house would change—and I didn't want what I and the landlord had already established compromised in some way. So, in partnership with him, we took it upon ourselves to find a new tenant that would be acceptable to both of us. To be perfectly honest, had the landlord not lived in the house, finding the perfect tenant might not have meant as much. As the owner, the landlord had a vested interest in maintaining the feeling of togetherness and tranquility he already had. I knew that the landlord would take care of the house, and us, properly.

Until that point in my life, I'd never thought how much value that feeling of fellowship added to my flat and to my quality of life—that flat had become my home. And, going full circle, added value to the landlord's sense of security and well-being as well. What he'd fostered over the years was, to all of us in the house, a huge win-win. So, finding a suitable tenant became a priority.

At first, the search felt quite daunting. I'd never sought a tenant before—I was, after all, on the opposite side of the equation, and the landlord had only done this a few times himself (due to low turnover). We were both new to this. But we came to realize that we had, through our connections with friends and family, work, and play, quite an established network. Because we knew more about those people than a quick check could establish, once someone came forward expressing an interest in renting, we knew they'd fit in. And, in turn, they knew they'd be welcome and have an already-in-place sense of community and safety that they'd actively preserve for their own benefit.

I only moved away from that first apartment because my husband and I needed more room than a flat could provide. But I took with me the knowledge that I'd spent several years without undo worry about where I lived, how that apartment would be maintained, or if I would be adversely impacted by other tenants. It was a wonderful and cool place to live during that phase of my life, and I look back quite nostalgically on all the great experiences we all shared.

CASE SUMMARY

You may also choose to only rent to those you know, like family and friends that are known to be trustworthy. With proper screening you can find great residents. Our Online Learning Portal will teach you how. Choosing responsibly at the very beginning will ensure autonomy and stability later.

From personal experience, the most critical part of choosing a tenant is the screening of applicants. The only time I've ever had an issue was my fault—I didn't meet the person at their current living location. Doing so would have alerted me to the issues that would arise later. I simply rented an empty unit over the phone. The rush to get it rented was my mistake. Do not skip that step.

The Business of Being a Landlord

Millions of people are landlords. The number of units they own span a range from one to thousands. The information on how to best do that is widely known and easily found.

The first shift when buying a home to subdivide, or carve out a rental unit from an existing property, is the mindset shift. You need to treat this as a business, with a business mindset and a sound business plan. In the beginning, you may feel alone. But the culture of ADUs is changing rapidly. Widespread acceptance is not far off. The Self Funding House™ online learning portal is available if you need assistance.

Landlords are small business owners. Their business is renting out housing. Likely, as an owner, you'll be the only 'employee.' Therefore, you'll be expected to fill multiple roles for the business to succeed. However, most of the roles are the same as a typical non-renting home owner. In addition, you'll be searching for good tenants when needed, collecting rents, and looking after the business aspects of the business. These roles are all positive ones and don't take too much time from your regular activities. In fact, most of the time, you'll be living much the same as if you were a tenant in your own home.

Some tips:

- For anyone who's applied for a student loan and managed a college budget, administering a rental business budget will be simple.
- Collection of rent is best done via direct deposit–eliminating the need to collect the rent manually or waiting for a check to clear.
- It's best to maintain a mostly hands-off relationship between landlord and tenant. They'll come to you if they need help. But like you, they value their privacy.
- Professionals are available for everything, including taxes, finding qualified tenants, rental administration, maintenance, lawn upkeep, and snow removal. A rental management company will do much of the administration for you and help keep the relationship on a professional level.
- In a co-ownership scenario, having a partner with complementary skills helps getting everything done right because the skills that you may lack are well developed in your partner.
- If you work from home, you can write off part of your housing costs. Buy a house that allows your tenants to work from home so they can take advantage of that too. It makes it a more attractive house for them.
- Focus on the kind of tenant you want so you can design the units to suit their needs. A unit designed for everyone will be difficult to rent. One designed for the targeted tenant will rent easily and command a higher price.

You're a Winner

I remember what a boost my first house gave me, and I want you to enjoy that experience too—it's life-changing!

Once you tap into your strengths and learn the skills that are necessary to run a business, the once-daunting tasks become quite manageable. There are plenty of resources available to learn the home ownership business and plenty more to help you select great tenants.

THE SELF FUNDING HOUSE™ ENTREPRENEUR MEMBERSHIP

ONLINE LEARNING PORTAL

TheSelfFundingHouse.com

Check out the course on *Business Ownership Basics*

When you take the initiative and get started, you'll feel like a champion, a victor, a winner. This leads to increased confidence which will permeate throughout all aspects of your life. You will become business savvy, fearless, and eager to take on new tasks and new challenges.

Responsible for your own life, you'll ensure yourself financial and housing stability—it gives you a huge advantage in the world. Much of a person's worry revolves around career, housing, and finances. As a landlord, you've met all three challenges and given yourself a massive head start—not to mention an opportunity to grow that one house into additional investment properties which generate ongoing income.

I can say unequivocally, that buying that house and converting it into a triplex shaped my success to a huge degree. I'd like to see you succeed as well—I know you can!

8

Wake Up Your Dream

"The people who are crazy enough to think they can change the world are the ones who do."
– Steve Jobs

Introduction

With an action plan in place, and a sound business plan that confirms the numbers do work, it's time to move forward and actually put everything into motion.

PLAN THE WORK—WORK THE PLAN

This is not the time to wait for the world to change for you. That's not you. You have dreams and goals, a clear path to make them reality, and you've committed to go after them. From now on, you're fully in charge of your future.

Adapt and Keep Motivated

It's all good that you're motivated to buy a house, start your business, and have the willpower to back that up. But it's not going to be quite enough, even though you've heard that advice countless times from those you trust. Every one of us knows that motivation is hard to maintain, even for something as important as buying a first home.

Think of what happens to most people when they join a health club. A huge percentage drop out after a short time. Sure, the reason for going is critical enough, but still, after a few weeks they're skipping days.

ADAPT TO STAY MOTIVATED

The key to staying motivated is to adapt to the hurdles that come your way and lean on that business plan you've carefully crafted. Achieving your goals isn't all about keeping the excitement levels up. Inevitable deviations from the plan will occur, but you're prepared for them. You learn, adapt, and keep moving forward one step at a time.

Start small and relish your small successes. Once you're past the first few steps, you'll realize getting past them is a major win. It means you don't have to do that part again. It means you've accomplished something that furthers your goals, and it feeds your motivation, so you don't run out of steam.

I want to remind readers that buying a home-as-a-business is not for everyone. It's for those whose mind is open to buying a house-as-a-business. It's for that younger person who has a housing affordability challenge and is willing to consider accessory dwelling units (ADUs) as sources of extra income.

> ***"Legends aren't defined by their successes; they are defined by how they react to their failures."***
> ***– Chris Bosh***

For those who want to see their dreams of home ownership come to life, buying a house-as-a-business opens so many doors—financially, professionally, and personally. It's hard to resist, and all with manageable business risk.

Your Plan
Within a Plan Within a Plan

YOUR ACTION PLAN

This is where you state your dreams, your goals, and what you're doing for the rest of your life. It begins now and ends well past retirement—maybe into the next generation. It gives shape to how you want to live your life and provides the framework to do what's necessary for life fulfillment and happiness. Sit down and write out your life action plan—and stick to it.

THE BUSINESS PLAN

Your business plan outlines everything you need to do to ensure your dream of buying a house-as-a-business becomes a reality. Each step requires little motivation, just some effort. But after a while, they add up.

If you've reached the point where you're ready to place an offer, do so. Whether you get the house or not is immaterial—but you have tried. If you do get it, now the excitement really ramps up and motivation is no longer a problem. But keep that business plan close. There's still more to do. Yet, you've tackled a seemingly insurmountable challenge, accomplished part of it, and are working on getting through the last series of steps. Things now look doable. The plan says it is—trust it.

Those who succeed know that small goals fuel bigger ones. It creates momentum and generates positive changes within you. It also cements the mindset change you've undergone. You now realize that you can meet your goals and that buying a house-as-a-business does indeed work—because you've proven it.

THE NUMBERS PLAN

The numbers plan is extremely focused. It's the nitty-gritty of the purchase of your first house-as-a-business, and then reappears as you buy more houses. It provides proof that your plan will work, giving you the confidence to make an offer, and satisfy investors and lenders that the purchase is sound.

Trust your plans—trust your dreams.

By trusting your plans you've offloaded much of the worry by building a sound framework supporting actions that lead to success. You now have the confidence to act decisively. You know how the action will end before you begin, leading to the payoff you've been anticipating.

TheSelfFundingHouse.com

Assembling the knowledge, wisdom, and content from many collaborators and industry experts, this Online Learning Portal will address the basic steps and solutions to challenges for buying a home-as-a-business and creating your **Self Funding House™**.

The Grand Payoff

The home ownership business is transformative and results in confidence that spreads across all aspects of your life. With a secure income source and a higher level of financial security, you'll soon see that new opportunities are yours for the taking. Your confidence has soared, allowing you to meet challenges successfully.

When looking at the longer term, you're no longer fretting about financial freedom. Instead, you're poised to take buying a house-as-a-business to a new level, seeing your first home as a career move, and thinking owning more houses (existing or new) means more and more income.

Everything about your life has been transformed, your finances, your business, and your life as a whole. Looking back, you'll see that buying that first house was the most significant move you'd ever made.

I know this is true because I have experienced it and I know how much that first house positively influenced my own life. I urge you to follow my lead and become successful in your own right.

9

Make Your Future What You Want It To Be

"My dream is for you to become the success you've always dreamed about."
– Derek Lobo

Where Change Comes From

If you want to create a cultural mind shift, it must begin at the top. In my day, drinking and driving was commonplace. Today, we wouldn't think of doing it. The culture around drunk driving has changed. We don't want to endure the consequences, whether they be potential accidents, injuries, or liabilities for allowing another to drink and drive. We now take a cab, Uber, Lyft, or have a designated driver take us home. My mind has been shifted and the minds of others have as well. But it took time, encouragement and education from a variety of sources.

Now, what if we said it's no longer acceptable for there to be a housing affordability crisis. Currently, many feel that the government should fix it. But what if everyone, celebrities, sport stars, politicians, corporate leaders, influencers, and most importantly, you and I, said that this is not how we want to live. We can do better. If we influence a change in our culture, we can make housing scarcity disappear. And yes, there's lots of talk about this issue at the moment, but no one seems to have a workable solution.

HOWEVER, I DO! AND NOW YOU DO TOO!

This book, along with others in this series, and the information found in The Self Funding House™ online learning portal are the solution. The reason readers will follow my advice and solve housing affordability (as opposed to affordable housing) is not only to help their fellow person, but to help themselves.

Remember, this book is for those who want to buy a house in a changing marketplace by thinking differently and leveraging the shared economy concept. However, the result is threefold: personal financial freedom, potential career opportunities, and long-term societal benefits.

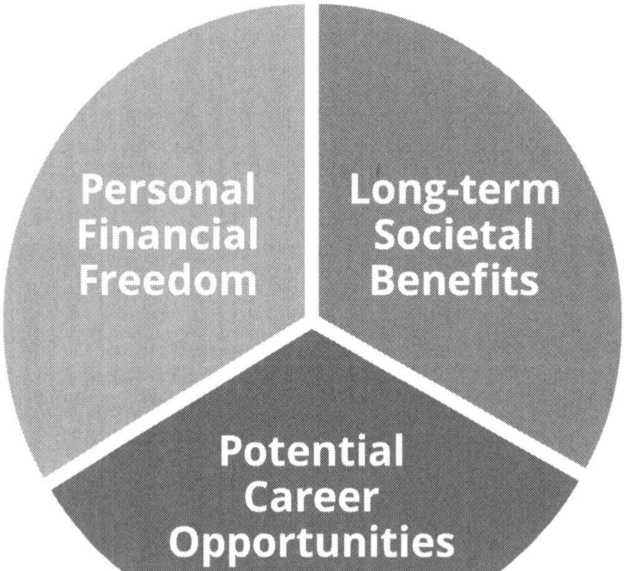

The result of buying a **Self Funding House™** is threefold: Personal Financial Freedom, Long-term Societal Benefits, and Potential Career Opportunities.

Adaptability Is Pure Confidence

Adaptability isn't resilience: resilience lets you recover; adaptability enables progress beyond recovery. Those with an adaptable mindset are continuous learners and have proven to be more resilient, happier, more creative, and more productive. High achievers are comfortable with failure. When others hit a wall, they make an excuse or give up. High achievers know that the only thing that keeps them from reaching their goals is to stop trying—so they don't, and neither will you. You know that you'll encounter obstacles and setbacks, but you won't be deterred. Your mindset has mentally prepared you for failure—you know it's coming, and it doesn't scare you or make you give up. You seek feedback, make changes, and get back into the game.

YOUR BUSINESS PLAN TO THE RESCUE

Give yourself permission to fail—it will take the pressure off getting a perfect end result. Your dream hasn't changed and your drive to succeed is still intact. Pursue your dreams as your action and business plans prescribe. Though you may put in 20 offers before one gets accepted, that acceptance, now or next week, is as valuable as any—and a huge win for you.

Who Are You?

Remember, changing your mindset doesn't happen by accident. It happens by choice.

If you're one of those who really wants to buy a house in today's changing marketplace, get ready to embrace your creative thinking and the shared economy. Home ownership for younger buyers is possible. Doing so opens the door to further business opportunities.

Your key is to buy a house-as-a-business and your willingness to utilize ADUs as extra income.

Even though we currently have housing supply issues and housing costs have skyrocketed, this book shows you it can be done. I know the process works—I've done it. And many are doing it now. Others who have witnessed me go through that process have duplicated that success for themselves—and I'm confident you can do it too.

Adaptability makes you powerful. The readiness to change your perspective from being blocked to making the obstacle part of the solution opens so many doors to progress. *The less you fear the challenges, the quicker they become paths to opportunities.*

Try these strategies:

- Be willing to adjust your plan. Changing course when it makes sense gives you control.
- Be open to the next opportunity. If one presents itself out of the blue, seize the opportunity to advance; others may just let it slide by. Being able to make those quick decisions increases your likelihood of success.
- Look forward, sideways, and back. Be on the alert for trends and changes in business direction. Be curious and ask others about the trends they've noticed. And pounce on an opportunity when it comes.

Remember, the playing field is level. Others may only see challenges, but by adjusting and adapting, you'll not only meet these challenges, but you'll also profit from them. In doing so, you'll feel the pride that home ownership and financial freedom brings. Revel in your success!

10

The Self Funding House™ Online Learning Portal

This book would not be complete without the needed resources and expertise to help take you to the next steps on your journey forward. I have learned many valuable lessons from my coach, Dan Sullivan, and one of those key lessons is about surrounding yourself with experts in areas that are not your core competencies (thus keeping yourself focused on your unique abilities). So why is this important? This principle is what I've used in bringing together experts in many fields needed for completing The Self Funding House™ project. These experts are contributing to creating a valuable online resource for people like you who want to implement The Self Funding House™.

TheSelfFundingHouse.com

This online resource is known as The Self Funding House™ Online Learning Portal, and you've seen it referenced throughout the book. It is filled with supporting information along with a myriad of additional content that supports all facets of business ownership, purchasing, executing, renovating, hiring, doing it yourself, renting, and living in your Self Funding House™.

Throughout my decades of real estate hands-on experience, I have developed relationships and collaborations with experts in a variety of supporting fields. The Self Funding House™ online learning portal features many industry experts and collaborators who have the knowledge and tools to help walk you through the process. I've collected this talent and made it accessible to you—the knowledge, skills, tools, and strategies to do it on your own or hire out. These online assets will continue to grow as we move forward.

When you first arrive at **TheSelfFundingHouse.com**, check out the FREE *Dreamer Membership* content and I'm sure you'll soon see what you have at your fingertips!

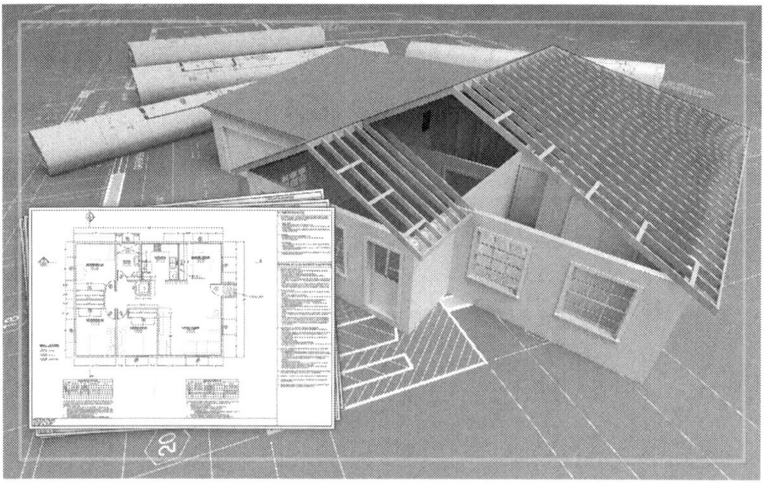

The Self Funding House™ Entrepreneur Membership
Plan – Buy – Implement – Grow

What Next?

The next book in this series is focused on the "how to" aspects of creating your Self Funding House™. Think of it as your blueprint for making your house a business. Even as I write this book, this project keeps growing and impacting the lives and business of many others, both inside and outside of the home industry. The third book is in the works too, focusing on the key stakeholders in the whole affordable housing dilemma.

I continue to make this my mission, to tackle the housing crisis head-on, and not sit back and wait for the government to solve this for us. We can collectively mobilize an army—an army of homeowners to start righting the ship of this global housing crisis.

Why?

Because it is the right thing to do!

Terms & Definitions

ADU (Accessory Dwelling Unit)

Self-contained apartments, secondary suites or residential units that are located on a property that has a separate main residential unit. An ADU can be attached to a principal dwelling, or can be a separate unit, located above a garage or in the backyard.

action plan

A document that lists the necessary steps to be taken in order to achieve a specific goal.

business plan

A document containing the goals of a business, the methods for attaining those goals, and the time-frame for the achievement of the goals. It also describes the nature of the business, background information on the organization, financial projections, and the strategies intended to implement the stated targets.

Dreamer Membership

The free membership to the Self Funding House™ Online Learning Portal, containing additional resources to help you own your Self Funding House™.

Entrepreneur Membership

The premium membership to the Self Funding House™ Online Learning Portal, containing additional resources to help you own your Self Funding House™.

equity

The monetary value of a property or business after debts have been subtracted.

house-as-a-business

A house that is being used to generate income through the rental of additional units. The owner of the property is acting as a landlord and is responsible for maintaining the unit(s), collecting rent, and providing services to the tenant. This can be an effective way for the owner to generate additional income and make use of underutilized space on their property.

mindset

A set of attitudes and beliefs that shape how a person makes sense of the world and themselves.

mind shift

The process of a person's mind changing from one way of thinking to a different way of thinking.

numbers plan

A detailed breakdown of the income and costs relating to your Self Funding House™. A numbers plan provides proof that your Self Funding House™ will be viable—giving you the confidence to make an offer, as well as proving to investors and lenders that the purchase is sound.

Online Learning Portal

A digital destination for learning everything necessary to own your Self Funding House™—including tools, financial models, floor plan samples, best practices, and information collected from a variety of experts in their fields.

secondary unit

Synonymous with ADU (accessory dwelling unit).

shared economy

A model of consumption based on the exchange, sharing, and collaboration between individuals of goods, services, resources, time, or knowledge via dedicated platforms.

zoning

Local codes regulating the use and development of property.

Resources

TheSelfFundingHouse.com
Online Learning Portal of resources for implementing The Self Funding House™ concept.

Business Plan Checklist

1. Go to TheSelfFundingHouse.com
2. Register for the FREE Dreamer Membership
3. Go to *Business Plan Checklist for Your Self Funding House™*
4. Download the checklist

TheSelfFundingHouseBook.com
The homepage for this book, complete with author biography, content, and purchasing information.

Financial Models
Various financial models for the planning of your Self Funding House™ are on the following pages. More detailed models are available in The Self Funding House™ Online Learning Portal.

LIVE / RENT

FINANCIAL MODEL FOR:
Owner occupies main floor - basement unit rented

HOUSE PURCHASE	Total Purchase Price	**$250,000**
	Down Payment (%)	**20%**
	Down Payment	**$50,000**
	Renovation Budget - Basement ADU	**$75,000**
RENTAL INCOME	Rental Rate *(LOWER UNIT)*	**$1,500**
	Utilities Charged *(LOWER UNIT)*	**$56**
	Rental Income *(ANNUAL)*	**$18,672**
MORTGAGE & EXPENSES	Mortgage *(MONTHLY)* 5.5% Interest	**$1,135**
	Mortgage *(ANNUAL)*	**$13,620**
	Additional Expenses *(ANNUAL)*	**$13,031**
	TOTAL EXPENSES *(ANNUAL)*	**$26,651**
NET OPERATING INCOME*	NOI *(ANNUAL)*	**-$7,983**
	NOI *(MONTHLY)*	**-$665**
	Required Household Income**	**$26,610**

RENT / LIVE

FINANCIAL MODEL FOR:
Owner occupies basement unit - main floor rented

HOUSE PURCHASE	Total Purchase Price	**$250,000**
	Down Payment (%)	**20%**
	Down Payment	**$50,000**
	Renovation Budget - Basement ADU	**$75,000**
RENTAL INCOME	Rental Rate *(UPPER UNIT)*	**$2,900**
	Utilities Charged *(UPPER UNIT)*	**$169**
	Rental Income *(ANNUAL)*	**$36,828**
MORTGAGE & EXPENSES	Mortgage *(MONTHLY)* 5.5% Interest	**$1,135**
	Mortgage *(ANNUAL)*	**$13,620**
	Additional Expenses *(ANNUAL)*	**$13,031**
	TOTAL EXPENSES *(ANNUAL)*	**$26,651**
NET OPERATING INCOME*	NOI *(ANNUAL)*	**$10,167**
	NOI *(MONTHLY)*	**$847**
	Required Household Income**	**$0**

** NOI = (Net Operating Income) What you're paying to live in the house and own it*
*** Based on 30% of annual income for housing (guideline)*

LIVE
RENT

FINANCIAL MODEL FOR:
Owner occupies main floor - basement unit rented

HOUSE PURCHASE	Total Purchase Price	**$500,000**
	Down Payment (%)	**20%**
	Down Payment	**$100,000**
	Renovation Budget - Basement ADU	**$75,000**
RENTAL INCOME	Rental Rate *(LOWER UNIT)*	**$1,500**
	Utilities Charged *(LOWER UNIT)*	**$56**
	Rental Income *(ANNUAL)*	**$18,672**
MORTGAGE & EXPENSES	Mortgage *(MONTHLY)* 5.5% Interest	**$2,271**
	Mortgage *(ANNUAL)*	**$27,254**
	Additional Expenses *(ANNUAL)*	**$13,031**
	TOTAL EXPENSES *(ANNUAL)*	**$40,285**
NET OPERATING INCOME*	NOI *(ANNUAL)*	**-$21,610**
	NOI *(MONTHLY)*	**-$1,801**
	Required Household Income**	**$72,033**

RENT
LIVE

FINANCIAL MODEL FOR:
Owner occupies basement unit - main floor rented

HOUSE PURCHASE	Total Purchase Price	**$500,000**
	Down Payment (%)	**20%**
	Down Payment	**$100,000**
	Renovation Budget - Basement ADU	**$75,000**
RENTAL INCOME	Rental Rate *(UPPER UNIT)*	**$2,900**
	Utilities Charged *(UPPER UNIT)*	**$169**
	Rental Income *(ANNUAL)*	**$36,828**
MORTGAGE & EXPENSES	Mortgage *(MONTHLY)* 5.5% Interest	**$2,271**
	Mortgage *(ANNUAL)*	**$27,254**
	Additional Expenses *(ANNUAL)*	**$13,031**
	TOTAL EXPENSES *(ANNUAL)*	**$40,285**
NET OPERATING INCOME*	NOI *(ANNUAL)*	**-$3,460**
	NOI *(MONTHLY)*	**-$288**
	Required Household Income**	**$11,533**

** NOI = (Net Operating Income) What you're paying to live in the house and own it*
*** Based on 30% of annual income for housing (guideline)*

FINANCIAL MODEL FOR:
Owner occupies main floor - basement unit rented

LIVE / RENT

HOUSE PURCHASE	Total Purchase Price	**$750,000**
	Down Payment (%)	**20%**
	Down Payment	**$150,000**
	Renovation Budget - Basement ADU	**$75,000**
RENTAL INCOME	Rental Rate *(LOWER UNIT)*	**$1,500**
	Utilities Charged *(LOWER UNIT)*	**$56**
	Rental Income *(ANNUAL)*	**$18,672**
MORTGAGE & EXPENSES	Mortgage *(MONTHLY)* 5.5% Interest	**$3,407**
	Mortgage *(ANNUAL)*	**$40,881**
	Additional Expenses *(ANNUAL)*	**$13,031**
	TOTAL EXPENSES *(ANNUAL)*	**$53,912**
NET OPERATING INCOME*	NOI *(ANNUAL)*	**-$35,237**
	NOI *(MONTHLY)*	**-$2,936**
	Required Household Income**	**$117,457**

FINANCIAL MODEL FOR:
Owner occupies basement unit - main floor rented

RENT / LIVE

HOUSE PURCHASE	Total Purchase Price	**$750,000**
	Down Payment (%)	**20%**
	Down Payment	**$150,000**
	Renovation Budget - Basement ADU	**$75,000**
RENTAL INCOME	Rental Rate *(UPPER UNIT)*	**$2,900**
	Utilities Charged *(UPPER UNIT)*	**$169**
	Rental Income *(ANNUAL)*	**$36,828**
MORTGAGE & EXPENSES	Mortgage *(MONTHLY)* 5.5% Interest	**$3,407**
	Mortgage *(ANNUAL)*	**$40,881**
	Additional Expenses *(ANNUAL)*	**$13,031**
	TOTAL EXPENSES *(ANNUAL)*	**$53,912**
NET OPERATING INCOME*	NOI *(ANNUAL)*	**-$17,087**
	NOI *(MONTHLY)*	**-$1,424**
	Required Household Income**	**$56,957**

** NOI = (Net Operating Income) What you're paying to live in the house and own it*
*** Based on 30% of annual income for housing (guideline)*

FINANCIAL MODEL FOR:
Owner occupies main floor - basement unit rented

HOUSE PURCHASE	Total Purchase Price	**$1,000,000**
	Down Payment (%)	**20%**
	Down Payment	**$200,000**
	Renovation Budget - Basement ADU	**$75,000**
RENTAL INCOME	Rental Rate *(LOWER UNIT)*	**$1,500**
	Utilities Charged *(LOWER UNIT)*	**$56**
	Rental Income *(ANNUAL)*	**$18,672**
MORTGAGE & EXPENSES	Mortgage *(MONTHLY)* 5.5% Interest	**$4,542**
	Mortgage *(ANNUAL)*	**$54,508**
	Additional Expenses *(ANNUAL)*	**$13,031**
	TOTAL EXPENSES *(ANNUAL)*	**$67,539**
NET OPERATING INCOME*	NOI *(ANNUAL)*	**-$48,864**
	NOI *(MONTHLY)*	**-$4,072**
	Required Household Income**	**$162,880**

FINANCIAL MODEL FOR:
Owner occupies basement unit - main floor rented

HOUSE PURCHASE	Total Purchase Price	**$1,000,000**
	Down Payment (%)	**20%**
	Down Payment	**$200,000**
	Renovation Budget - Basement ADU	**$75,000**
RENTAL INCOME	Rental Rate *(UPPER UNIT)*	**$2,900**
	Utilities Charged *(UPPER UNIT)*	**$169**
	Rental Income *(ANNUAL)*	**$36,828**
MORTGAGE & EXPENSES	Mortgage *(MONTHLY)* 5.5% Interest	**$4,542**
	Mortgage *(ANNUAL)*	**$54,508**
	Additional Expenses *(ANNUAL)*	**$13,031**
	TOTAL EXPENSES *(ANNUAL)*	**$67,539**
NET OPERATING INCOME*	NOI *(ANNUAL)*	**-$30,714**
	NOI *(MONTHLY)*	**-$2,560**
	Required Household Income**	**$102,380**

** NOI = (Net Operating Income) What you're paying to live in the house and own it*

*** Based on 30% of annual income for housing (guideline)*

Financing Solutions

One of the first questions a first-time home buyer needs to answer is, "*How much capital do you have to begin with?*" Capital shortage is the number one item that prevents you from moving forward with home ownership. The amount of capital you have determines what size of house or extent of renovation you'll be able to take on at the beginning.

If you only have a small down payment, it might make more sense to purchase an already-completed turn-key cash flowing property as you only need to put a small percentage down as a first-time home buyer. If you purchase a fixer-upper property, you will need to inject a larger sum of capital in order to complete the renovations to get the cash flow started, which could be 6 to 10 months later. There are some good options to help you fill the gap between the capital you have and what you'll need.

Here are a few (among many) options to fill the gap:

1. **FAMILY:**
   Money from parents, aunts/uncles, grandparents, etc.
2. **PURCHASE PLUS IMPROVEMENTS MORTGAGE:**
   Speak to a mortgage broker about a "*purchase plus improvements*" mortgage where the renovation capital is provided as part of the initial mortgage and paid out in draws as the renovation work is completed. This is a very common approach for first-time homebuyers.

3. **ALTERNATIVE FINANCING:**
   Speak to a mortgage broker about "*alternative financing options.*" That is, B Lenders or private lenders. A private lender is a private individual who loans money via the mortgage broker. In some cases, you can get more capital from someone else and put less of your own money into it. You do pay a higher interest rate and it's something you should consult with a professional mortgage broker about.

4. **VENDOR TAKE-BACK MORTGAGE (VTB):**
   Ask the seller of the house if they would provide a VTB. An existing homeowner (the seller) who has owned their home for a long time and decides to sell it could very well have a lot of equity in the home. Instead of getting a mortgage from the bank for the entire purchase price, the seller continues to hold a portion of the purchase price in a "*vendor take-back mortgage.*" This would result in you requiring less money from the bank which means an even smaller down payment is required. In some cases, you can get up to a 90%-100% vendor take-back mortgage and require very little of your own money to put down.

5. **ACTIVE PARTNER:**
   Offer yourself as the "*active partner*" in a joint venture with another more passive "*money partner.*" You split the ownership of the property 50/50. In this scenario, you may not have to put any money into it. You are contributing your time and expertise in exchange for the other partner contributing the capital. You split the profits 50/50.

6. **SIDE HUSTLE:**
   In addition to your full-time job, start a side hustle that will help generate more income so that you can save quicker. There are countless examples of people who have a "*side hustle*" in addition to their regular jobs. This could be freelancing, a small business, an online store, reselling Amazon products, drop shipping, odd jobs, direct sales, etc. The possibilities are endless.

About the Author

Derek Lobo is called the *"Apartment Guru"* because of his decades of speaking, writing, consulting, brokerage transactions, relationships, amortized knowledge, and industry wisdom. He is one of the most connected individuals in the apartment industry, living by his personal motto: *always stay in traffic!*

As a student of new apartment construction, student housing, and affordable housing, Derek has established a sterling reputation and industry credibility as an expert advisor in these fields. To date, he has authored eighteen books and is the visionary behind the *Apartment University* online learning portal and *The Self Funding House*™.

Firmly established as a *"thought leader"*, Derek's unwavering mission is to impact one of the world's greatest challenges—the lack of rental housing. His *Apartment Development FULL Service Experience*™ brokerage firm continues to serve landowners, financiers, developers, and apartment building owners.

Now in his fifth decade of business, Derek continues to be an *"Apartment Collaborator"*, by bringing together like-minded, talented individuals to solve business challenges and create opportunities. His keen insight and strategies have allowed him to broker some of the nation's largest and most complex real estate transactions. He is currently the Broker of Record and CEO of SVN Rock Advisors Inc., Brokerage.

My Notes

My Notes

Manufactured by Amazon.ca
Bolton, ON

34180009R00068